JULIA CLEMENTS

Flower Arranging
for
All Occasions

JULIA CLEMENTS

Flower Arranging
for
All Occasions

BROCKHAMPTON PRESS

LONDON

A CASSELL BOOK

First published
1993 by Cassell
Villiers House
41/47 Strand
London
WC2N 5JE

Reprinted 1993

This edition published 1998 by Brockhampton Press,
a member of Hodder Headline PLC Group

ISBN 1 86019 8856

Printed at Oriental Press, Dubai, U.A.E.

British Library Cataloguing-in-Publication Data
A catalogue record for this book is available from
the British Library

Typeset by RGM Typesetting, Southport

Contents

Introduction

Everyone loves flowers; they are part of our lives from the moment we are born until we die. They give us a chance to express ourselves, whether we are at home or are celebrating an occasion such as a birthday, anniversary, wedding or party – in fact, there is not an occasion during the year when flowers cannot play their part.

So important are they that I often feel they should have a star role. It is not always enough that flowers be placed on a table – because by habit that is where we usually stand them – but they should be elevated to play an important part, no matter what event is planned.

Flowers are often taken for granted, but they are living expressions of ourselves, for they have come from a seed, just as we have, and although their lips are silent, they can play just as significant a role at every celebration as we can with all our finery. They can prove their importance with their colour, shape or scent, but no matter how you allow them into your event, please do let them make an impact.

There are several kinds of flower arrangers, and it is never easy to please everyone, but I am sure, whatever your tastes, that you will find something of interest in this book, even if it is only words of encouragement to those wanting to make a start.

Some people want nothing more than to place the flowers from their gardens in vases so that they can enjoy the beauty and fragrance indoors. The sections on picking and conditioning flowers will be of help here. Others are fascinated by the art of flower arranging and want to learn about design, rhythm, transition, the use of colour and so forth, a knowledge of which is essential for more ambitious arrangements. Still others may wish to compete at shows and exhibitions; such people need a thorough understanding of every aspect of flower arranging as well as of different shapes, sizes and forms of plant material. People who wish to enter exhibitions and shows must also be familiar with all the competition regulations. Some people are called upon to provide floral decorations for functions and grand events, where lavish displays of a kind not appropriate for the average home are required.

Do remember: there is no mystery about flower arranging; everyone can do it – it is just the idea of taking the first steps that can be a bit off-putting. But, if you place just five flowers, one below the other, on a pin-holder in a low dish and fill the dish with marbles or stones instead of simply plonking the flowers in an upright vase, you have made a start, and you will never look back.

This book is not meant to show all the latest designs or newest gimmicks, for these come and go. Rather, I hope it will encourage you all, whether you are a beginner or have been arranging flowers for several years, to use and enjoy flowers on every possible occasion.

CHAPTER ONE

Choosing Your Flowers

Flowers grow in many shapes, colours and sizes. Some are single blooms, others grow in sprays, while some are made up of small florets that form one large spike or flower. 'What shall I pick?' or 'What shall I buy?' are the questions many people ask when they are planning a flower arrangement for the first time. It may be that friends are arriving and you wish to decorate your rooms with fresh flowers to give the house a 'lived-in' and welcoming atmosphere. It may be that you just love flowers and want to become more efficient at arranging them, or it may be that you have not been able to resist a brightly coloured bunch of flowers from the florist. Whatever the reason, take heart, for there are tips to be learned to help you not only with the arrangements themselves but also with the selection of your flowers.

You are lucky if you have a garden that provides you with flowers for cutting, but everyone at some time or another finds it necessary to buy flowers from a florist. This may be because it is a season of the year when flowers are scarce in the garden, and, if so, they will be expensive because they will have been grown under glass or imported. Another reason for visiting a florist may be that you need a particular variety of flower for a special occasion, such as a wedding reception or a cocktail party.

Search around until you find a florist's shop you can rely on and where you know the flowers will be fresh. It is often a false economy to buy cheap flowers, because these can be beyond their prime and will not last. A busy, fashionable florist's shop may seem daunting, but in any shop that has a fast turnover the flowers will be fresh. If you make friends with your florist and show that you have a genuine interest in flowers, you will find that he or she is very willing to assist you and offer helpful advice.

Always inspect the flowers carefully before you buy them. The petals should not be damaged or have any bruise marks on the edges or in the centres, and they should feel crisp when felt between your fingers (although this can depend very much on the variety). The flowers should have a good, strong, natural colour and must show no signs of fading. Check flowers that have a mass of petals to see that the centres are tight and not fully open. The foliage is another indication that flowers are in peak condition; fresh foliage should not appear to be wilting or turning yellow or brown. The stems should be crisp and green, not black and slimy, when they are removed from their water. Remember, too, that flowers that have been forced will not last as long as those that have grown outside and in their correct season.

Late spring flowers, including rhododendrons and sprays of flowering Deutzia, *were used in this arrangement for a sideboard. Always establish the height and width of an arrangement before you begin to fill in the shape with larger blooms.*

This low arrangement, which was used on a coffee table, was composed of winter leaves and sprays of ivy picked from the garden, with some grapes and purple anemones added to provide colour contrast. The stems were held in a well-holder on a green base.

Late summer flowers are here grouped closely together for a hall table. Roses, lilies, campanulas and phlox made this colourful group held in place with water-soaked floral foam. The flowers were purposely not placed flowing forward due to lack of space.

This arrangement, which would be suitable for a low side-table, was composed of golden privet, to give width, with creamy hydrangeas in the centre. Additional foliage – here, sprigs of Lonicera nitida 'Baggesen's Gold' – was added to fill out the shape forwards and backwards. The low dish was filled with floral foam to hold the stems securely.

When you cut flowers from your garden, try to pick them when they are not in full bloom. Experience will show at what stage to cut the different varieties so that they last as long as possible once they are brought into the house. It is also important to pick the flowers so that the plant will benefit and not be affected any more than is necessary. Try to leave as many buds on the plant as possible and to pick long stems with several flowers on them. Make sure that the buds are showing the colour of the flowers; green, tight buds will not open in water. Plants that bear an abundance of flowers throughout the season will benefit from heavy picking, which encourages new growth and the production of more flowers.

Many beginners wonder whether the vase comes first or the flowers. I would say, rather, that it is the setting. Before you select a container or the flowers, you should study where the arrangement is going to be placed, and this will help you to decide on the type of vase or container and, finally, lead you to the correct choice of flowers and foliage. For instance, if your room is fairly large and you want to make an impressive arrangement for a party, you will need an important container that will lend itself to tall flowers. On the other hand, should you wish your dining-table to sparkle and to be the centre of attraction, you will need to choose shorter stemmed flowers, so that the arrangement will be low, and to include trailing foliage to stretch out at the sides to make a horizontally styled design. Pittosporum, eucalyptus, lonicera or ivy are all good leaves for the sides of a low table arrangement, and the centre could then be filled in with carnations, roses, sweet peas or any shorter flowers. Gladioli would not be the best choice for a table arrangement, although I have cut the stems shorter, using the tips for the width and the wide open florets for the centre.

Let us look at what to pick or buy for a *large* arrangement that would be suitable for a party or wedding reception or for filling a large space. You will need a selection of different sizes, shapes and forms to make an interesting design. Flowers that are all the same size and length, just put in a vase, will not appear very artistic.

It will help if you think of the three main stages of flower arranging when you select your flowers. First, you need tall and thin flowers to form the outlines of the arrangement; delphiniums, lythrum (loosestrife), with its dense, star-shaped flowers forming tall spires, gladioli, golden rod, antirrhinums or forsythia, or leaves such as eucalyptus, lonicera or pittosporum are useful here. Fine grasses, bare branches, budded sprays and the green foliage and flowers or berries of berberis also come into the 'outline' category.

Second, you will need to use clusters of berries or even a cluster of small flowers in the centre of interest; large leaves or materials of a heavier texture can also be included. The centre of interest is usually placed at the base of the tallest stem, and it is from this point that all the stems should appear to emerge.

The final stage is to fill in, and here medium sized and less important flowers are used – scabious, spray pinks, spray chrysanthemums, daisies, love-in-a-mist, geums and aquilegias to name but a few. You will also need some leaves to give depth and to place around the centre to unite the stems, and perhaps some trails of ivy or periwinkle to flow downwards, so uniting the flowers to the container.

If you are faced with the problem of having flowers all of one kind and size, the answer is to follow the same idea as for a mixed selection. Cut the flowers to different lengths, using the long stems for the outline, the medium length stems for filling in and the shorter, yet larger, flowers for the centre. If the arrangement requires a dominant centre, you can cluster a few blooms together or add some grapes, pine cones, leaves or berries, depending on the season and what is available. For a more modern design you could use a bare branch or piece of wood for height and larger flowers low down for the main interest. Large leaves, such as bergenia, hosta (plantain lily) or fatsia, could be used in between.

It is important to buy or pick flowers that are in scale and proportion to the vase in which they are to be placed, just as it is important that the vase is in proportion to the setting in which it will stand. Small, delicate vases made from china or glass will fit well on a side-table under a lamp when they are filled with small flowers such as pinks, cornflowers or freesias, with their funnel-shaped flowers and beautiful fragrance. If the arrangement is to be placed in a high position – on a mantelshelf or wall sconce, for example – try to include honeysuckle, ivy or periwinkle to trail downwards. Narrow, tall vases will fit in well with high-ceilinged rooms and tall-stemmed flowers, but if the setting is a cosy room with a low-beamed ceiling the arrangement should be shorter and more rounded.

It is not only the form, shape and size of the flowers that must be considered but also the colour. If the walls of the room are dark, light coloured flowers will show up far better, whereas if the room is light in appearance, greater effect will be gained from using dark, strong colours. Personal preference will, of course, enter into the decision of what you pick or buy, but whatever your choice, try to obtain flowers of different sizes and shapes, even if they are all the same colour.

Experience will soon help you to assess how many stems you will need for an arrangement. For a fairly large design I usually pick or buy nine tall stems for the outline, seven large round flowers to place at the centre of interest and approximately twelve medium-sized stems for filling in and flowing forwards low over the rim. I like to include a spray of leaves for the background, some bolder leaves, such as hosta, bergenia or peony, around the centre and a few trails for the sides and the front. However, before the flowers are arranged they must be conditioned, for no one wants to create a work of art with flowers, only to find them drooping the next day.

No flower arranger can function without leaves, for although you can always buy flowers if your garden does not provide sufficient for your needs, you can seldom buy foliage in the size, shape or colour you require for particular designs. I have listed here a few of the shrubs that I would not be without, although, rather like selecting my 'Desert Island Discs', I find it hard to confine myself to just a few.

All the shrubs that follow are evergreen and, when the plants are well established, they will not mind being cut. Until they are well established, remember to cut above a leaf joint and to take from the back or from underneath. If you are going to use a lot of foliage, plant a few extra shrubs at the back of the vegetable plot!

We all need tall, spiky leaves for the background of our arrangements and some rounded shrubs for filling in, while a few flat leaves to give depth around the centre of a design are always welcome. The following selection should meet these requirements.

- *Aucuba variegata* (spotted laurel). This shrub is truly a cut-and-come-again plant, and its evergreen spotted leaves are ideal for brightening up winter arrangements. Use it with white, yellow and bronze flowers, especially around the centre where you need to focus attention.
- *Choisya ternata* (Mexican orange). I love this plant. It offers round heads of glossy green leaves, which are perfect for filling in and for covering the 'mechanics'. Deliciously fragrant flowers appear in the spring.
- *Cornus alba* 'Elegantissima'. Whenever you need sprays of green and white leaves for a wedding or church arrangement, this is the

shrub. Let it spread and enjoy the leaves.
- *Eleagnus pungens* 'Maculata'. This golden-splashed evergreen shrub is a must. The stems last well when cut, and they are ideal for placing with the bare stalks of daffodils to make an interesting design.
- *Euonymus fortunei* var. *radicans* 'Silver Queen'. The glossy, cream-edged leaves will light up the centre of any display.
- *Fatsia japonica* (Japanese aralia). The large, palmate leaves, with their thick stems, are ideal for modern designs and for the background of some large arrangements.
- *Ligustrum* 'Aureum' (golden privet). When this is well established, do not trim it as you would a hedge, for the long, golden stems are ideal for the outline of all types of arrangement, and they show up well in churches.
- *Lonicera nitida*. This fast-growing shrub gives long, thin stems that are suitable for outlines, modern designs and for table decorations. The variety 'Baggesen's Gold' has golden leaves.
- *Senecio laxifolius* (sometimes sold as *S. greyi*). A low-growing, silvery-grey shrub that seems to withstand all weathers and gives leaves that are the perfect accompaniment for pink, mauve and crimson arrangements.
- *Viburnum tinus* (laurustinus). The round heads of duller green leaves can be placed between bare stems in the centre of an arrangement. There is the added bonus of pinkish-white flowers in late winter and early spring. A bowl of cuttings from this shrub in winter warrants its inclusion in any garden.

Gardeners will tell you that there is plenty of variety in the garden, even in the depths of winter. The shrubs used here included, at the top, some spikes of the yellow stars of Cornus mas *(cornelian cherry), with some pussy willow and stems of* Eleagnus pungens *'Maculata' to give height. Hanging down at the left were the tassel-like catkins of* Garrya elliptica, *and these were balanced on the right by the creamy heads of* Pieris japonica. *In the centre were some blooms of the pale green* Helleborus argutifolius (H. corsicus), *while under these and to the left were some flowering sprays of* Viburnum tinus (laurustinus). *The vase was filled with crumpled wire netting to hold the stems in place.*

Although they are not shrubs, most flower arrangers will need the leaves of the following from time to time.

- *Arum italicum.* These delightful arrow-shaped leaves are marbled with creamy-white veins, and they appear in the autumn. Although this is a moderately tender plant, it is well worth the effort.
- *Bergenia cordifolia.* This low-growing evergreen plant has roundish, glossy and slightly fleshy leaves that are ideal for uniting bare stems in modern arrangements.

The variety 'Purpurea' has lovely maroon-bronze leaves.

- *Hosta* (plantain lily, funkia). There are many varieties of this broad-leaved plant that are worth growing. They are an arranger's delight. The clumps die down in the winter, to appear again in the spring.

These are just a few of my own particular favourites, but, as you attend flower shows and visit other people's gardens, look out for the colours, shapes and sizes that are used and introduce the plants you think you will use most often into your own garden.

CHAPTER TWO

Looking after Cut Flowers

Whatever flowers you have chosen, you will find that they will last longer if they are conditioned before you arrange them. This applies to all cut flowers, whether they have been picked from the garden or bought from a florist or whether they are received as a gift. The temptation to arrange the flowers immediately must be resisted so that your hard work and design will give pleasure for the longest time possible.

Different types of flowers require different types of conditioning, but as soon as any flower or foliage is picked it is deprived of its natural source of water, and the sooner it is put into water the longer it will last. Here are some suggestions to help you condition your flowers, remembering that much depends on when and under what conditions the flowers were picked.

Remember always to pick flowers before they are fully mature, and, whenever possible, pick flowers at night or early in the morning, when loss of water is at its lowest. During the day flowers lose water by evaporation, through the process of transpiration.

When you pick flowers from your own garden, take a bucket filled with water so that the stems can be placed in water as soon as they are cut. If you are picking wild flowers, they should be immediately wrapped in wet newspaper or polythene. This will keep them fresh on the journey home. As soon as you arrive home, re-cut the stems and place the flowers in deep water overnight.

All flowers should have the lower leaves stripped off the stems, which should be re-cut under water. This is particularly important for hollow-stemmed plants as it will prevent an airlock forming in the stem which will stop the flower from taking water. The stems should be cut at an angle, which will create a wider exposed area than a straight horizontal cut and will allow the flower to take in the maximum amount of water. The angle-cut stem, when placed in a vase, will rest on the lower point of the angled cut. A flat-ended stem would lie flush with the bottom of the vase, obstructing the flow of water up the stem. The re-cut flowers should be left in deep water overnight in a dark, airy place before being arranged. This treatment will harden the stems and allow the flowers to become fully loaded with water.

All woody-stemmed flowers, such as lilac, viburnum, outdoor chrysanthemums, roses and other flowering trees and shrubs, should have some of their lower leaves removed and the bottom 1½in. (4cm) of their stems split or crushed before they are placed in deep water. I prefer to split the ends because crushing causes bruising and allows bacteria to form. Using a sharp knife or florist's scissors, scrape off the

Lilac (Syringa) is now available in several colours, including primrose. Remove the lower leaves, re-cut and split the stem ends and stand in deep water for several hours before arranging. Crumpled wire netting held the stems in place for this triangular design. Chrysal powder or a teaspoonful of sugar in the water helps lilac.

lower 1½in. (4cm) of the outside covering (the bark) of the stem to expose the inner tissue. Split the exposed stem lengthwise.

Always remove the white portion at the stem ends of bulbous flowers, such as early tulips and daffodils, as they drink only from the green portion.

Hold the stem ends of plants such as daffodils and hyacinths under warm running water to remove the sticky sap they exude. If this is not done, the sap forms a seal over the end of the stem and makes it more difficult for the flower to take in water.

Jointed stems, such as those of carnations and sweet Williams, should be cut at an angle just above one of the joints.

Certain flowers – delphiniums and lupins, for example – will benefit if the hollow stems are filled with water after cutting and then plugged with cotton wool before being left overnight in deep water.

Lupins are best picked when only the three lower rings of florets are open. The stems should be cut straight, not at an angle. This helps the lupin spires to remain straight, because they have a tendency to bend.

Some flowers – dahlias, poppies, and euphorbias, for example – exude a white substance called latex when they are picked, and this will quickly form an impenetrable skin over the end of the stem, depriving the flower of water. This can be avoided if the cut stem ends are allowed to stand in 2in. (5cm) of very hot water for about 10 seconds. Alternatively, the ends can be singed by holding them in a flame for a few seconds. Both these methods disperse the latex layer and stop any further flow.

Roses will last longer if the lower leaves and thorns are removed and the stem ends split before they are placed in water. Wilting roses, which have been left out of water for some time or have arrived by post, should be treated in the same way before being placed in near-boiling water to which a teaspoon of sugar has been

Three gourds (or calabashes) were rubbed all over with grate polish to form this conversation piece for a modern room. The calabashes were placed on a black base and the red carnations were held in a well-holder.

added. There are also several commercial products, such as Chrysal, which can be added to the water instead of sugar and which will revive wilting flowers. Most flowers will last longer if sugar is added to the water in the container in which they are arranged. (This does not apply to daffodils.) Use 1 teaspoon (5ml) of sugar to 1 pint (600ml) of water.

Tulips will always turn to face the light. Pierce the stem just under the head with a pin and then wrap them in newspaper so that the stem and flower are both well supported. Plunge the newspaper-wrapped flowers into deep water and leave overnight.

Hellebores and anemones will stand up strongly if a pin is drawn down the side of the stem from top to bottom before they are left to stand in deep tepid or warm water, prior to arranging.

Gourds, which form the basis of many dried arrangements, should be picked when they are fully ripe and the skins are hard. Try to leave a short stem on the gourd as this makes wiring easier, if it is needed. Place them on a sheet of newspaper in a warm room or cupboard to dry and remember to check them regularly and to wipe off any transpiration with a cloth.

Blossoming sprays can be forced into early flowering if they are first submerged in warm water to swell the buds and then, after slitting the stem ends, placed in warm water in a warm room. This will work only if the blossom is picked when the buds are swollen and ready to burst.

Mimosa (acacia) is not renowned for being long lasting, and it has a tendency to turn dark and lose its beautiful bright yellow colour. This can be avoided if it is kept in a polythene bag until it is needed. Just before it is required for arranging, dip the flowers first in cold water and then in hot. Mimosa will last longer if the stem ends are split and placed in 3in. (7.5cm) of near-boiling water to which 1 teaspoon (5ml) of sugar has been added. Adding one of the proprietary cut-flower powders to the water in which the flowers are to be arranged, will help them to live longer. Mimosa will not remain fluffy for long indoors, but even when it is dry it is still attractive.

Leaves and sprays of greenery should be submerged in water for some hours before they are arranged, but be careful, because if some leaves are soaked for too long they lose their texture. Only experience will tell you how long to soak different varieties of leaves. Do not soak leaves that have a woolly texture or that are heavily covered with hairs. Lamb's tongue is one of these varieties – it will soak up water like a sponge and, as a result, lose its beautiful grey tones. Dip the stems of woolly textured leaves into boiling water for one or two minutes, taking care to wrap the leaves in paper to protect them from the hot steam. The leaves should then be conditioned in shallow water.

If *Begonia rex* and other house plants with rather soft leaves are cut and used in decorations, they should first be submerged for some hours in water to which 1 teaspoon (5ml) of sugar has been added.

When you place flowers in deep water to condition them, make sure that the containers are spotlessly clean and are the correct size for the flowers. Do not place short-stemmed flowers in with long-stemmed ones, as these may crush the smaller flowers or drink so much water that the shorter stems are left clear of the water.

Always have warm water in the container or vase you are arranging into, as this will prevent the ends of the stems from drying while you work. A tablet of charcoal in the water will help to keep it pure. Check the level of the water every day and top it up with tepid water if necessary.

Keep all flower arrangements away from the hot sun and cold draughts, even if this means that you must move them from time to time. It will be worth it.

Exotic flowers, such as anthuriums, orchids and strelitzias, although very long lasting, will benefit if the stem ends are re-cut after a week to remove the brown stain that often appears. If it is allowed to remain it will attract bacteria.

A fine spray of water around the arrangement will help to counteract the loss of moisture through transpiration. These sprays can be purchased from garden centres and hardware shops. There are also several commercial products – Clear Life and S.100, for example – that can be sprayed lightly over the arrangement to close the pores of the plant material. This is particularly beneficial for arrangements in exhibitions and on occasions when the flowers must last for a long time.

The shine on camellia, rhododendron, laurel and other large-surfaced, shiny leaves can be prolonged if they are wiped over occasionally with a damp cloth sprinkled with a few drops of oil. There is also a commercial product, available from florists and garden centres, which does the same job.

When you use floral foam to hold the flowers in place, make sure that it has been well saturated with water. This will take about 30 minutes. Leave a space at the back of the vase where more water can be added daily.

The only way to perfect the conditioning of flowers is to experiment, but remember:

- cut the stems of all flowers under water and then leave the flowers to stand in deep water for several hours in a dark, dry and airy place before arranging them;
- split all woody stems;
- submerge most leaves in water for a few hours before using them;
- use tepid water in your container and top it up every day.

If you follow these rules, your flowers should stay fresh and be a source of joy to all who see them.

CHAPTER THREE

The Tools You Will Need

To make a start with flower arranging you need only three items: a pair of florist's or kitchen scissors; a pin-holder, a piece of wire netting or some floral foam; and a container, vase or dish.

However, as you progress you will find that, just as a good cook requires a number of different implements or an artist requires various brushes and paints, you will need more items to enable you to create various styles for different occasions. So let us look at some of the items a good flower arranger will use.

HOLDERS

Holders are very important, for it is almost impossible to make a well-designed picture with flowers unless you use some kind of holder to keep the flowers firmly in place.

Pin-holders

Flower pin-holders are an essential piece of a flower arranger's equipment. They are made in many sizes and shapes, although the most common shape is circular, varying from 1in. (2.5cm) to 3in. (7.5cm) in diameter. Oval and rectangular pin-holders are also available. Pin-holders are mainly used in shallow dishes or to give extra support for the angled and heavy stems used in large, tall and wide arrangements.

Metal pin-holders have a number of closely packed nails held point upwards in a heavy lead base, and they can be obtained from most florists' shops, garden centres and department stores. It is also possible to obtain extra-heavy holders containing larger nails to hold weighty branches. Others have very fine, sharp pins, and these are suitable for flowers and foliage with especially thin and delicate stems, such as sweet peas, freesias and small spring flowers. By selecting the correct pin-holder, you will be able to fix any type of flower easily into the pattern you wish.

If you find your pin-holder is inclined to topple over, try fixing it firmly to the bottom of the container with plasticine or adhesive clay. Press three round knobs of plasticine or clay on to the dry base of the holder, then press it down on to the dry surface of the base of the dish, giving it a twist as you do so. Florists sell a special substance that will hold the pin-holder permanently in place, and this is ideal if you have a container that is used only for flower arranging. As you become more proficient at flower arranging you should not need plasticine to hold the pin-holder in place – if

A permanent background of dried twigs can be kept in a tall, narrow-necked vase. All that is needed is the addition of one round flower – a camellia, as here, or perhaps a rose or a dahlia.

your design is well balanced, as it should be, it will not overbalance. In the beginning, however, you will find plasticine very helpful.

Pin-holders are also useful in tall containers, especially the tubular sort that are so tall that the flowers placed in them fall to the bottom leaving only the heads visible. This can be overcome by filling two-thirds of the container with sand, then pouring hot candle wax over the surface to form a false platform. When the wax is set, the pin-holder can be placed on it. Alternatively, you could place the pin-holder in a shallow tin of water and stand this on the platform.

Pin-holders are not suitable for placing in clear glass containers as they can be seen through the glass. Instead, try using a small roll of crumpled wire netting at the top of the vase opening, or criss-cross the top with adhesive tape or florist's tape to form a grid. The ends of the tape should be cut just below the outer rim of the vase and held in place with a continuous length of tape stuck around the outer edge. The flowers and foliage can be inserted into the openings between the tape. Leaves and foliage can be trained over the rim of the vase to hide the wire or tape.

Well-holders
❊

A well-holder is a variation of the pin-holder; it is simply a pin-holder welded into a heavy, metal, shallow cup. The cup-like base holds the water, so that the well-holder can be used in shallow baskets, on flat bases or on other items that are to be placed behind an ornament or collection of fruits where it will be well hidden. A piece of water-soaked floral foam pressed on to the pins of the holder will add extra holding power when downward angles are required.

Well-holders are available in a variety of shapes and sizes. If not easily obtainable, a pin-holder, placed in a tin or plastic dish deep enough to allow water to cover the pins, will do equally well.

Wire Netting
❊

For upright, classical vases a piece of crumpled wire netting gives excellent support, as long as you push it well down into the vase and allow some of it to rise above the rim.

Wire netting can be obtained from most hardware shops where it is sold in yards or metres. A 2in. (5cm) mesh is the best for general use, although a finer mesh is more suitable for small flowers.

Cut the wire according to the size and shape of your container. If you mean to fill the vase completely it is best to have the wire netting twice the width and twice the height of the vase. It takes a little time to fix the wire netting firmly in the container, but it is time well spent. Make sure that it reaches just above the rim of the container, do not crumple it too tightly and leave a fair amount of space in the centre where most of the stems will meet.

You can press the cut ends of the mesh over the rim of the vase to hold the netting in place or thread string through the mesh at the edge of the container, pulling it tight and tying it around the top outer edge of the vase. If you are using a small container, two strong rubber bands passed over the top of the netting at right angles to one another and down under the base of the bowl will hold the netting firmly to the vase. Reel wire (see page 30) can be used for larger containers: use the wire in the same way as the rubber bands and secure it at the base by twisting the two loose ends of wire together.

I often use a pin-holder under wire netting to give added support to the stems, and I find that I can get the quickest and best results this way. This method is particularly useful for a tall container with a wide opening, such as a compote stand or an urn, because the stems placed vertically down through the wire and on to the pin-holder will be held firmly, while other stems can be inserted almost horizontally at the sides and the front of the container. I also use this method in a shallow cake tin, which I then place on a silver or white china cake-stand.

Cutting Tools

Scissors

Special flower or florist's scissors can be purchased from horticultural suppliers. These are not expensive and will prove to be a very good investment. They have short blades, one of which is serrated, and usually have a small notch at the base of the blades for cutting wire. If you take care of them and oil them regularly, these scissors will last a long time. Although you may think you can manage with ordinary scissors, you will often find that they will squash the stems of your flowers.

Secateurs

Most keen gardeners will possess a pair of secateurs, but although they are useful to flower arrangers for cutting extra-thick, strong branches, they are not essential. Wire cutters are also useful for cutting wire netting, stub wires and reel wire, and this will save your flower scissors, which otherwise would have to be used for this job.

Knives

A good sharp knife is useful for scraping and cleaning plant material, but it must be very sharp so that it makes a clean cut through stems and does not simply crush them. Remember to keep all sharp knives and pointed scissors out of the reach of children.

Buckets and Cans

Buckets

You will need a bucket to soak the stems of flowers that are being conditioned before arranging. It is best to have several different sizes, because small, short-stemmed flowers may be crushed if they are put to soak with larger flowers. Buckets with side handles are more practical than those with only one handle, as the handle may damage the blooms when the bucket is being carried. Try not to use your buckets for anything other than flowers and foliage because any trace of detergent will harm the flowers. Keep the buckets spotlessly clean and remove all traces of plant material when the flowers have finished soaking.

Watering Cans

The most useful kind of watering can is one with a long, thin spout, which will enable you to top up your flower arrangements without disturbing the flowers and foliage.

Cones and Candle Cups

Cones

Metal or plastic cones are invaluable when more height is needed in an arrangement than the tallest stems can give. This applies to pedestal groups for parties, weddings or church arrangements. Cones can be bought from garden centres, or your florist should be able to obtain them for you. They can

Cones are available from florists and garden centres, and they are invaluable when you need an especially tall arrangement. They can be fastened to bamboo canes and either filled with water or with pre-soaked floral foam.

be used singly, or you can attach several to a garden bamboo stick with adhesive tape or wire. The stick can then be inserted into floral foam or crumpled wire netting, whichever you are using. Several cones placed at different levels can be used. The cones should be filled with water or water-soaked floral foam before the flowers are inserted. Most cones are green, but you can spray-paint them any colour you wish to fit in with the colour scheme of your arrangement. Cones should, however, never be visible when the arrangement is finished.

Use reel wire to provide a false stem for pine cones and nuts that you want to include in arrangements or to lengthen short-stemmed leaves and flowers. Reel wire can also be used to strengthen fragile stems and stalks.

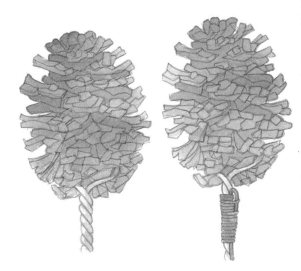

Candle Cups

These useful gadgets can be obtained from florists' shops, and they are made from plastic or metal. Plastic candle cups are usually gold, silver, black or white, but if none of these fits in with the colour of your container, they can be sprayed any shade with one of the many aerosol spray paints that are widely available.

Candle cups are shaped like a shallow bowl with a stem at the base, and they are mainly used in candlesticks, bottles or other narrow-necked containers. A piece of plasticine or modelling clay can be placed under the bowl part of the candle cup to hold it firmly in place.

WIRE

Reel Wire

This thin wire is sold on spools, and it is used for several different purposes in flower arranging. It can be used to secure crumpled wire netting to containers, and it is also used for wiring single leaves, pine cones, delicate florets or any plant material that has no stem. The wire provides a false stem as well as strengthening leaves and other floppy foliage. Reel wire is used when a group of stems needs to be bound together or attached to a garland or swag.

Stub Wires

These come in a variety of lengths ranging from 7 to 18in. (18–46cm). They also vary in thickness, and it is useful to have a mixed selection of thin, 22 gauge (0.71mm), medium, 20 gauge (0.90mm), and thick, 18 gauge (1.25mm), stub wires. Note that the lower the imperial gauge the thicker the wire and the lower the metric gauge the thinner the wire.

These wires are used mainly by florists, whose skills fashion lovely bouquets and corsages, but amateurs often need them to make false stems and to lengthen short-stemmed flowers. Always use a thickness of wire that is in scale with the flower or foliage you are wiring. A thick stub wire will rip through the delicate petals of a floret, while a thin wire will not have the strength to support a heavy bloom.

BASES

A base is any item on which a flower arrangement rests. It can be a flat, water-resistant mat to protect furniture, or something used to raise a flower arrangement. Today, with the worldwide increase in the popularity of flower arranging, a base can also be used to accent the colour of the flowers at a show. One or more thinner bases can be placed crosswise to each other to add a note of distinction.

FLORAL FOAMS

Floral foams, which can be bought under several brand names, are plastic substances that absorb water. The main difference between the various makes is in their density. Use a dense foam for heavy floral material and a lighter one for delicate stems. If you have difficulty inserting thin, soft stems into the foam, pierce it first with a fine knitting needle or bodkin. Foam comes in different sizes – it can be oblong, cylindrical or round. It is usually coloured green, which fits in

well with the foliage; foam in other colours than green is not always water absorbent and should be used only for dried arrangements. It is not always possible to buy foam that is the right size for your container, but a large piece can easily be cut to the correct size with a knife. Always cut the foam so that it sticks up above the rim of the container. Large vases do not necessarily have to be completely filled with foam and a piece wedged in the top of the container will hold the flowers in place.

Dry foam should be soaked in sufficient water to cover it, and it is ready to use when it starts to fill and sinks to the bottom. Leave the foam to soak until it is completely saturated; this should take about 30 minutes. Once it is full it can be placed in the container.

Although floral foam is not suitable for all arrangements, it is particularly useful for show work and for designs for special occasions. It has the great advantage of allowing you to place your flowers at any angle. Even flowers and foliage that swerve downwards will be held firmly in place while still being able to absorb moisture.

If the foam cracks and breaks up when heavy stems are inserted, use some other method or cover the foam with wire netting. When an extra-large piece of floral foam is needed for 'tree pots' or free-standing arrangements, two or more pieces can be held together with wire netting.

MOSS

Sphagnum moss is the moss most often used in flower arranging. It is used for lining hanging baskets, covering bowls of bulbs and concealing wire netting, pin-holders, cones and any other aid that needs hiding. It can also be used as a base for flowers as it holds moisture well. Sphagnum moss is found in woods and boggy land, and it can be kept fresh for a considerable length of time if it is soaked in water and stored in a polythene bag.

Three twigs of varying heights were first inserted into the pin-holder, which had been placed in the base of the pottery dish. Two white Anthuriums and a bergenia leaf created the central interest, while pieces of wood and some stones were used to cover the holder. Water was, of course, added to the dish.

A cone of floral foam was held securely on a large pin-holder standing in a wine cooler. One end of a short stick was inserted into the apples and the other end into the foam, which was completely hidden with short sprigs of foliage.

Club mosses (*Selaginella* spp.) are useful for placing on the surface of containers that are planted with pot plants which like plenty of water. If the moss is removed carefully from its natural growing place and placed on the compost around the plants it will continue to grow.

ℭONTAINERS

A flower container today can be almost any receptacle that will hold water. The word 'vase' is used mainly to describe tall, thin containers that are specifically made to hold long-stemmed flowers.

Wall brackets were probably the first containers to have been designed to hold flowers in the home. The first of these seem to have been produced by the Leeds Pottery in the mid-eighteenth century, and these were soon followed by salt-glazed stoneware brackets from the Staffordshire potteries. The famous Wedgwood factory made urn-shaped bough pots in 1770, a shape that is still popular among flower arrangers.

Today, the tremendous upsurge of interest in flower arranging means that a wide variety of containers can be bought. However, you will probably already have many suitable items in the home. They do not have to be traditional shapes but can include coffee pots, dishes, plates, cake-stands, glasses, goblets and bottles, as well as fine china and silverware. They can be made from metal, pewter, pottery, copper, wood or any other water-resistant material. Whatever you choose, it will have a role to play in holding flowers for a particular occasion.

Choosing a container is important, and as much care and attention should be given to this as to the choice of flowers. The container and the flowers must unite so that one does not dominate the other. The colour, texture, form and scale of the container should have as much interest as the

flowers and foliage that are to be placed in it. Another point to consider when you make your choice is the setting in which the flower-filled container will be placed. A tall, thin vase is not suitable for a coffee table – a china cup and saucer filled with delicate flowers would be much more fitting. Natural-coloured containers seem to unite well with most coloured flowers, but make sure that the shape fits in with the general style of your home.

The style of your design will also determine the shape of the container. An upright, classical container filled with crumpled wire netting will lend itself best to a formal mass arrangement, whereas a low, open dish used with a pin-holder is preferable for a modern, linear design. A tall tubular-shaped container is ideal for branches arranged in the Japanese style, while a wine glass will look effective simply filled with lilies-of-the-valley or similar flowers, which need no support and form an informal arrangement. Special flowers, such as orchids or roses, look especially elegant when they are arranged in fine china or silver containers.

Baskets

Baskets of all kinds have many uses for plant and flower arranging. The half-moon shaped shopping baskets, which can be hung from a wall or door, make ideal containers for pot plants. You can use them for flowers and foliage either by inserting a watertight container inside the basket or, if it is made with a close weave, by lining it with polythene and then wet floral foam. Flower arrangements in these types of baskets look especially attractive if stems of ivy or tradescantia are allowed to trail down over the edge of the basket.

By lining baskets with waterproof tins or dishes, old fishing creels, wicker bags, picnic hampers, basket-ware trays and even waste-paper baskets

Wicker-covered bottles were used as the basis for this modern arrangement, which was designed for a side table standing against a wall. The straggly pieces of dry roots were placed over the bottles first, then the chrysanthemums, some inserted into a well-holder low down. Some nuts were placed on the brown base to finish the composition.

become effective containers for fruit, flowers and leaves, particularly in a rustic setting. Even a summer straw hat or holiday coolie hat, up-turned and set on a table, will provide a good base for a plant or leaf grouping. In fact, there is endless potential for any form of basket woven from straw, rush or palm and used as flower and plant containers.

Shells

Shells make interesting containers for growing plants or for cut flowers and foliage, and their attractive interiors can sometimes be left uncovered. An empty shell, backed by sea lavender and grasses, can make an interesting arrangement. Sprays of silvery-grey *Artemisia absinthium* or of pink rosebay willowherb that has gone to seed, held on a pin-holder in the base of an upturned clam shell, can give the impression of plumes waving in the sea. Place the shell on a black wooden base or small tray to protect the furniture and add to the picture.

Flowers and foliage can be held firmly if the shell is packed with floral foam, moss or sand. Whichever method you use, make sure the filling is kept constantly wet. A giant shell can have a small, foam-filled container laid inside it and secured with plasticine, but be careful that the water does not spill out if the shell has curved lips or wavy edges.

Shells come in all shapes, sizes, colours and textures. The large green snail shells, which are iridescent on the outside and pearly inside, are so beautiful that it is a shame to place anything inside them but a few fine, tall, green sprays. These will not only give height but accentuate the beauty of the shell. Small shells of any kind can be placed in the shallow water around the base of a pin-holder to make interesting underwater decorations.

Line the inside of the shells with two coats of varnish to help make them watertight. Fill with floral foam to hold the flowers or grasses (alternatively, the foam can be wrapped in plastic).

Common scallop shells are not to be shunned either. They can make delightful individual place setting arrangements or be grouped together for a table centre-piece. To do this, mix some plaster filler powder with water to make a thick consistency. Pile this on to a base and insert into it five scallop shells, arranging them in a circle near the base; next, place three shells slightly higher and nearer the centre of the pile of filler, rather like the petals of a flower. Finally place a single shell on the top. The shells can be filled with flowers and foliage or with small sedum or echeveria plants.

Bottles

Bottles make fascinating containers. Stone cider and pickling jars filled with wheat, grasses and berries in the autumn can look attractive placed on an old oak or pine dresser.

Dark green wine bottles and decanters should be washed out well and scrubbed inside with a bottle brush. If the bottle is made from clear glass, a few drops of vegetable food colouring added to the water will look attractive and will also help to conceal the stems. Small bottles, such as old scent bottles or small old blue or clear glass medicine bottles, when used in conjunction with small flowers and feather-like foliage and placed on a dressing-table or bedside cupboard in a guest room, are a welcoming sight to visitors.

Making Your Own Containers

More adventurous arrangers can experiment with making their own containers. Tall or shallow round biscuit tins can be painted with a mixture of paint and sawdust, which gives a rough-textured finish. Alternatively, rush table mats can be glued around them.

Tins of all shapes and sizes can be converted into useful containers. Cement, which can be purchased from hardware stores in small bags, can be mixed with clear glossy or matt varnish or gloss paint. This mixture can be spread on to the outside of the tins. The paint or varnish helps the cement to adhere to the smooth surface. To vary the texture of the surface, imprints of buttons and other small objects can be made by pressing them into the wet surface of the cement. If the wet cement is stroked on to the outside of the tin with a fork, it will give the appearance of ridged wood. Pastel colours can be obtained by adding a few drops of coloured ink or food colouring to white plaster powder.

There is a wide variety of patterned tins on the market, but if you cannot find one of a suitable colour you can always paint it yourself. In fact, you can paint any metal or enamel pieces of kitchen equipment a different colour – colanders, old kettles, weighing scales and old bread bins could all be given a new lease of life. I once painted a metal colander with mauve paint, planting it later with pink and purple petunias and hanging it over my studio door.

You can even mould an old gramophone record into a container if you soak it in very hot water to soften it. Seal the central hole with hot wax to make it watertight.

Another idea is to make a raised base, using four cotton reels and a piece of wood 18×12in. (45×30cm). Nail or glue the cotton reels to the wood, approximately 2in. (5cm) in from the corners. Screw or nail an empty tin to the top of this home-made table, either in the centre or to one side. Paint the whole thing with matt black paint. If you coat the tin with vinegar and allow it to dry before painting it, the paint will more readily adhere to the tin. Place a smaller tin inside the tin nailed to the wood to make it watertight.

You can use a bottle, a cork and a tin pie-dish to make a container that will look most attractive when it is filled with short-stemmed flowers and drooping foliage. Screw or nail the cork to the

centre of the underside of the tin. Drop candle-grease or sealing wax round the nail to stop water leaking through. Weight the bottle by filling it with water or gravel, then insert the cork into the neck of the bottle. The flowers and foliage can then be arranged in the tin.

*D*RIFTWOOD AND BARK
❀

Driftwood can be turned into a container as well as being used as a base or incorporated into a design. All wood that has been weathered by rain, wind or snow is called driftwood; the word does not apply only to wood that has been in the sea.

Wash the wood well, scrubbing it with a solution of detergent, disinfectant and water, then put it to dry in a warm place. Once it is dry it can be trimmed into the shape you require with a knife or, if the branches are thick, with a small saw. The loose bark must be scraped off, but if you wish to have the branch without any bark at all, soak it in water for a few days before scraping it. Because the driftwood will have been lying exposed to the elements, it will more than likely have a few rotten patches where the wood has turned soft. These areas can be scraped out and the hole lined with foil or polythene to make a container for flowers. If the wood will not stand steadily on a surface, it will have to be secured to a wooden base with a large screw through the base of the wood and into the driftwood.

If the piece of driftwood is large, it may be better to secure it to a tin or a wooden base with plaster of Paris. The plaster should be mixed with water to form a stiff paste. Pile this in the centre of the base or on to the tin and, working quickly, press the driftwood into the plaster. Paint the tin and the plaster a neutral shade so that it fits in well with the colour of the driftwood.

Bark can make a natural, textured container. A large, intact, semicircular piece of bark can be lined with foil or polythene and then filled with moss or floral foam. This type of container fits in well with a country setting.

*P*LANTERS

❀

Containers are not used just for flower arranging but also for plants. These containers can be delicate or coarse – glass or silver for delicate plants such as the maidenhair fern, and wood or pottery for more robust leaves and seedheads. Baskets also make ideal containers for mixed groups of plants, while copper, brass and pewter are often the best choice for leaves and plants that have a similar colouring. A plant of lamb's tongue (*Stachys byzantina* syn. *S. lanata*), transferred from the garden to a pewter mug, can make an inexpensive and appealing decoration on a writing desk, while *Grevillea robusta* (silk oak or Australian wattle), with its fern-like leaves, will have a ravishing and long-lasting effect if placed in a copper or brass container.

The various combinations are endless and time spent in the search for new ideas is often very rewarding.

Wood is very effective in modern settings. Here, a heavy piece of wood was spray-painted and placed on a black base. The back was completely covered with purple statice, which was held in a well-holder filled with foam. Some of the flowers peeped through to be seen at the front, although the arrangement was viewable from both the back and the front. No after-care was necessary, making this an ideal arrangement for someone who has little time to spend replacing dead and drooping blooms.

CHAPTER FOUR

Flowers For the Home

When you bring flowers into your home you are expressing a facet of your own character. You may be a gardener and want to display the flowers you grow; you may choose to use pink flowers to complement the pale green walls of your room; but whatever you use, the flowers will certainly bring your home to life. Whether you place a brightly coloured group in the hall to greet friends or a pastel-coloured posy in the bedroom to charm a guest, the flowers will never go unnoticed.

Finding new ways of using flowers to complement different room settings offers you an exciting opportunity to project your own personality through the creative use of colour or the individual style of the arrangement. The warm, bright, advancing colours such as yellow, orange and red will give a certain gaiety or welcome in a dark hall whereas mauve, blue or purple (which are receding colours) would hardly be noticed in dark surroundings. Conversely, mauve or blue colours would be ideal in a bedroom. But, however you use your flowers, always put a little of your heart and personal style into arranging them. Even informal arrangements of flowers in kitchens or bathrooms will give more pleasure if you have taken care over the selection of flowers and choice of container. Remember that it is not only your own enjoyment in arranging flowers that is important, but the great pleasure you give to others who see them.

INFORMAL ARRANGEMENTS

Informality means not striving for effect, but allowing the flowers to look natural and true-to-life in their container. There are no fixed rules for an informal arrangement; it need not consist of a studied colour scheme, nor, indeed, have any particular design. A perfect informal arrangement need not rely on the use of mechanics; the flowers should support each other with the help of the edges of the container. This is not, of course, always possible, and the choice is left very much to the individual. Whether the arrangement consists of a bunch of mixed flowers from the garden or is the result of picking bits and pieces from the hedgerows, the casualness and air of simplicity add delightful charm to any home.

At the same time, what may appear pleasantly informal in one home may not be so in another. For instance, a bunch of marigolds set in a pewter tankard would appear informal and very acceptable in many settings, but it would not look so lovely if it were set on a fine antique table in an elegant period house. So, although there are no set rules, the surroundings and background of any arrangement must be taken into account.

Containers for informal arrangements should be simple and basic, but they must still unite with the

A black pottery vase was used for this informal arrangement of lilies and peonies, which stood on a coffee table. Sprays of hazy gypsophila were added to complete the overall effect. On this occasion no holder was needed.

Roses, picked in the garden, were arranged informally in a delicate china container. Floral foam was used to hold the rose stems in place and to enable the trailing stems of plants such as honey-suckle to be positioned so that they trail downwards. Remember that rose stems should be re-cut after picking and the flowers should be left standing in deep water for several hours before being used in an arrangement.

An informal yet charming way of displaying small posies of your favourite flowers is to place them in dainty glass vases. No holder is needed for the stems.

A basket of mixed fruit and vegetables is all you need for a simple yet effective decoration for a kitchen table. Mushrooms, artichokes, tomatoes, grapes, aubergines, pineapple and courgettes all have different colours and textures.

flowers. All kinds of kitchen utensils – storage jars, kitchen scales, copper kettles and saucepans, for example – can be used. Glass food containers and vases are excellent as they can be found in a wide variety of simple shapes and sizes. Stone pickling jars and cider bottles are ideal for bunches of flowers. Loosely tie three or four bunches together, pulling up some flowers to make sure that all the heads are not standing together, and insert these into the jar so that the heads come just above the rim. Such a colour-block of flowers, inserted in a tubular container, would look most attractive placed under a table lamp. A wine glass painted with iridescent nail varnish or car spray paint and filled with dainty flowers, such as pinks, will make an eye-catching arrangement. Cups and saucers can make interesting containers, and wine bottles are a never-ending source of delight. Stand a wine bottle in a wine cooler, insert a candle into the top of the bottle and fill the cooler with short-stemmed flowers for an unusual display. It is these little effects and changing ideas that give such satisfaction – so open your eyes and try something different.

Flowers for everyday use need not be so studied as those for special occasions. Yet your imagination can be given full play as you look around the home. It is not only in living-rooms, dining-rooms and entrance halls that flower arrangements are

Freesias and sprigs of heather were grouped in a pretty shell-shaped container for this arrangement, which would be ideal for a bedside table.

This formal triangular arrangement was made from annual flowers, grown from seed sown in the garden in the spring. All flowers should be given a long, deep drink before being arranged in floral foam.

Using different shades of a single colour can be extremely effective. Here, pink Alstromerias, roses, pinks and fuchsias were arranged in an elegant silver container.

appropriate. With the trend towards country kitchens it is very acceptable to have flowers or foliage on display. These must fit in with the general décor and style of the kitchen and be placed so as not to interfere with the preparation of food. Place flowers on one side of a pair of kitchen scales and balance the other side with various fruits. If your scales are of the modern type, a casual arrangement of flowers and foliage can be placed in the weighing tray.

A large jug filled with stalks of corn, barley and deep blue cornflowers or a few poppies, of which there is a wide range to choose from, will make a suitable arrangement. Poppies make a beautiful informal arrangement on their own. Iceland poppies (*Papaver nudicaule*) are the best kind for cut flowers, and their tissue-paper-like textured flowers are borne on leafless stems. They come in a wide range of different colours, including mixtures of reds, pinks, oranges and yellows. You must remember to seal the stem ends in the flame of a match or in boiling water if you want them to last. It is also best to pick them when they are in bud, but make sure that some colour is showing, because all-green buds will not open once they are cut.

A bunch of all-white flowers placed in a simple white china container would be as suitable for a country kitchen as for an austere, modern formica one. Simple flowers, such as daisies, marguerites (*Chrysanthemum frutescens*) or ox-eye daisies (*Leucanthemum vulgare*) are all ideal.

Bathrooms can also look most attractive with flower arrangements in them. A carefully placed posy of flowers or some colourful plants arranged along a window-sill can make all the difference to this room, which can often look rather cold. The arrangements can be of either dried or fresh flowers. Pampas grasses placed in a tall container standing on the floor can make a long-lasting display, which will look especially fine in a dark bathroom as the pale, fluffy plumes will stand out against a dark background. If you place flowers in front of a mirror or mirror tiling, you will have to arrange them symmetrically because they will be reflected in the mirror. Try placing a single rose or bloom in a long-stemmed container for the side of a wash basin or shelf. Groups of potted plants also look very effective in bathrooms, and most varieties will thrive in the warm, humid atmosphere.

Bedroom flower arrangements should blend in with the decoration of the room, and they must be placed so that they cannot be knocked over in the dark. Delicate flowers are suitable for most bedrooms, so make good use of pastel colours. Sweet peas, freesias or delicately coloured irises such as 'Blue Denim', are all suitable. These can be placed on window-sills, bedside tables or dressing-tables.

THE TRADITIONAL STYLE

❊

The traditional or classical style of using plenty of flowers loosely arranged with flowing lines to gain effect is typically British. Make sure that your container blends happily with your room and furniture, and remember that the shape of your arrangement should suit its position in the room.

A formal, massed triangular shape is ideal for the centre of a table that is backed by a wall, whereas an irregularly shaped mass design – that is, one that is shorter on one side than the other – is better for one end of a similar table. This off-centre style is often used at one or both ends of a mantelshelf, especially at wedding receptions.

Formal designs call for formal vases, so avoid heavy, shallow pottery dishes of the kind that are so necessary for modern designs, and use instead your best silver, glass or fine china containers, filled with exquisite blooms. Flowers such as sweet peas, roses, lilies, orchids, delphiniums and the more choice flowers are considered suitable for formal flower arrangements. Colour is also important in formal displays. Mauve, purple, pink, crimson, blue and other delicate colours are all suitable; bright red or harsh yellows, on the other

Delphiniums were used to give height to this formal pedestal arrangement of summer flowers. Flowing foliage was used to provide width, while heads of pink kalmia and lilies formed the main interest and pinks were used as fillers. The large bowl was filled with floral foam covered with chicken wire to hold the stems in position.

This formal living-room arrangement was composed of campanulas, cerise stocks, peonies and roses. The cache pot or bowl was filled with crumpled wire netting, although floral foam would have done just as well, and the thinner stemmed flowers were inserted first to form the overall low triangular shape.

Whether you are making an asymmetrical or a symmetrical arrangement, you must position the main outline flowers first. For an asymmetrical design (right), begin by placing the tallest stem towards the right of the container. The tallest flower in a symmetrical arrangement (left) should be placed in the centre, with the shorter blooms and foliage emerging from the base.

hand, are not always the ideal choice. Small, fine containers filled with tiny, precious flowers and leaves lend an air of formality, especially when they are placed on antique furniture, perhaps under a lamp. Large traditional triangular arrangements are often used in churches and at weddings. You must always make sure the flowers flow loosely and forwards over the rim, for if they are closely packed they will appear as a blob from the back of the church (see Chapter 6).

To make a formal triangular arrangement, position the flowers that are to form the outline first. Then decide where the arrangement will finally stand, making it taller if rooms are high, shorter if low. For large, high rooms use a fairly large vase, for nothing offends the eye more than a large mass of flowers in a small vase. Only when you are happy with the overall proportions should you add the blooms. That will be the centre of

interest and, last of all, the foliage and flowers that you have chosen to fill in the shape.

For an asymmetrical mass formal design, start by placing the tallest stem off-centre at the left, adding large leaves and flowers at the left and longer, finer ones low at the right. For an 'all round bowl' of flowers, start with five stems like an outstretched hand, with the first one in the centre. The rest of the flowers should be cut shorter and point forwards until, near the rim, some will flow out and over the rim. Turn the bowl round and fill up the back as in the front. Should the effect appear too full and even, add a few pointed stems here and there to lighten the effect. You will find that each time you attempt an all-round bowl, large or small, it becomes easier. But remember, the final effect should be 'in' and 'out', i.e. heavier flowers 'in' near the foam or wire and light, pointed flowers 'out'.

These flowers, including pinks, roses and mauve hostas, were inserted into wet floral foam, which was held in a dish that was itself placed on a china cake-stand. Arrangements of this kind are suitable for living-rooms.

Red tulips provided the main interest in this modern design for a modern setting. The container was half-filled with crumpled wire netting, and the dry root was placed across the opening. A stem of ivy and some dry broom were added, and finally the tulips were inserted through the wire into the water.

A modern design can be made of two, three or five stems of flowers placed one below the other on to a pin-holder standing in a pottery dish. In this arrangement a piece of wood was placed across the opening of the dish before the sprays of lilies and three stems of dry fasciated willow were added.

THE MODERN STYLE

If you live in a house or flat of contemporary design you will probably be most interested in the modern style of flower arrangement. Although often appearing more bold and exciting than traditional styles, successful flower arrangements in the modern manner are, in my opinion, easier to achieve.

To make an original modern design do not be afraid to use strong or contrasting colours; neither must you fear heights, for tall designs are more modern than squat ones. You must also learn to appreciate the value of space and allow for it around the principal lines of your design. Be careful to resist the temptation to fill up the spaces in your arrangement because you are afraid it might appear too sparse.

An appropriate background is most important. If your walls are pale, you can place before them dark branches and bright leaves; if they are dark, it would be better to use striking colours such as yellow, orange and scarlet.

The right container is also a matter for consideration. It should be plain and uncluttered in appearance, perhaps made of thick metal or pottery, and it can be shallow or tall, according to the space to be filled.

Although flowers alone can make interesting modern designs, a contrast of form will make the pattern more eye-catching. For instance, a tall branch with short flowers grouped low down, or tall flowers with a piece of gnarled wood placed low in the design, will prove more exciting than six flowers, all of one kind, placed upright in a container.

So if you are interested in making creative modern arrangements, now is the time to start looking for accessories that will be useful for adding a different shape or form to your design. Collect large stones, rough pieces of wood, old roots, dried fungus, shells and even ornaments, for all these are valuable accessories to modern flower arrangements. Pieces of wood can be sand-papered to obtain interesting textures, and other items may be rubbed smooth, polished with shoe polish and finished in a variety of colours.

The ideas are endless, but a strong, linear, uncluttered design that uses bold colours and strong forms will give the appearance of a modern design more than a mass of dainty flowers.

This modern design was composed of three stems of 'Star Gazer' lilies, which were inserted into a well-holder placed inside a black-painted wine-rack. Sprays of dainty gypsophila were added to lighten the effect.

This unusual design for a modern side-table was created with two contrasting textures. Two pieces of oak bole were placed, one on top of the other, while the delicate gypsophila was held in a holder tucked in at the back. This kind of arrangement can be left to dry in situ.

The centre point of this modern design of forsythia and pussy willow was formed with a few daffodils. The stems were held firm on a pin-holder placed in the base of the container, and a small piece of wood placed over the rim finished the effect.

The tall dracaena plant was left in its pot and placed in a large container. It was surrounded with soil into which further small plants were inserted. The pink tulips were placed in a cone of water, which was inserted between the plants.

Plants and Flowers

Many who live in towns or cities enjoy fresh flowers but cannot always give them the attention they require. A possible solution is to group together a number of pot plants, adding some fresh flowers, either in a tub of water or in a dish tucked in between the plants. Some call this a *Pot et Fleur* design, but this seems to me to be a misnomer, for it is, in fact, not 'containers and flowers', but 'plants and flowers'. However, whatever you call it, this method of decoration is certainly a very popular one. Many people use pot plants to decorate their homes, but, although they can be restful at times, it is easy to become tired of the constant green. So why not add a few cut flowers to your plants?

There are two main ways of making such a decoration. One is to use a container that is sufficiently large and deep to take several plants in their pots so that you can add small containers, tubes or blocks of floral foam between them to hold the cut flowers. The other method is to remove the plants from their pots and to re-arrange them in a container already prepared with crocks and soil, again leaving space for a few cut flowers.

I often use a third method, when I do not want to remove all my plants from their pots. I leave some in their pots, but remove one or two extra ones, wrapping their roots with a ball of moist soil enclosed in plastic, and these can easily be squeezed between the plants left in their pots. After a few weeks or more, those that have been removed from their pots can be unwrapped and re-potted in a little more fresh compost.

The method of making such a decoration is similar to that of creating a flower arrange-ment – you need different forms, shapes and sizes; some tall, some short and some trailing plants, for you will need height and depth and something to trail over the rim, and of course your added flowers will provide the focal interest.

It is advisable to use plants that have similar cultural needs, so that they can be watered *in situ*, and you should choose plants that thrive in shade or light for certain positions in a room. Of course, the arrangements can always be moved around, but it does not suit ferns or even ivies to be placed in full sun, whereas plants with variegated leaves enjoy sunlight.

There is no end to the variation of ideas that can be used when grouping plants, but the problem does arise of when and how often to water the plants. It is difficult to generalize, for many plants have different requirements, and in the beginning it is perhaps best to stay with three or four easy-to-care-for plants. However, a general instruction is *not* to overwater, for it is this that causes the roots to rot and the leaf tips to turn brown. Wait until the top soil looks a light brown and is dry, then you can water.

The plants can be left in place for weeks on end, provided they are watered and nourished when needed, but it is as well to remove them now and again and to spray them overhead with water – you can buy very effective mist sprays in most garden shops and centres; add a few spots of liquid fertilizer to the water about every 10 days in summer; less (even no) fertilizer in winter, and your plants should flourish for a very long time. Remember to protect furniture before you spray. So do try this idea for an unusual and economical home adornment.

Growing plants were used for this spring table decoration. The container was filled with gravel and soil, and into this were inserted hyacinths, daffodils, primulas and ivy to give a variety of heights. An arrangement such as this will last for a long time if it is watered occasionally.

Wilton House, Salisbury, was the setting for this group of plants and dahlias picked from the garden and arranged on the handsome William Kent console. The tall pinky-tan shrimp plant (Beloperone guttata) was added for height, while the variegated Ananas (pineapple) created the central interest. The plants were left in their pots, and the dahlias were held in floral foam in a dish.

CHAPTER FIVE

Parties and Celebrations

Parties! Everyone loves a party, so why not offer them as often as you can. It may be a birthday, a wedding anniversary, a home-coming, a cocktail or buffet party, a garden party or even one held specially to celebrate your favourite flowers. But whatever the reason, do let your flowers play a prominent part in the proceedings.

The flowers that you choose can help tell the story or play up the theme, so try to emphasize them. Birthday party flowers can complement the person whose birthday it is, so unless you are restricted to those growing in your own garden, do consult the person for his or her preferences. For a very young girl, you might use simple pink and white flowers. Try tying them in large bunches and place pink ribbons around the house. Remember that small flowers need to be bunched or they can be lost. I once made a tall arrangement of pink and white blooms that stood in the centre of the table and from it a pink ribbon streamer reached over to every place at the tea table. On the end of each length of ribbon was a small gift, and the little girls talked about it for a long while.

Teenagers need more sophisticated flowers. They are certain to have their own ideas – they might want bright colours combined with wood and all types of odd containers. They may want fruit and flowers or even colourful vegetables.

COCKTAIL PARTIES

Flowers should play an important part as decorations at a cocktail party, and if you exaggerate their use they can assume a star role. The flowers must be used profusely – display masses of them on mantelshelves, tables and pedestals so that they become the talk of the party and are remembered long after they have died.

If the party is held in the early part of the year, try using only mimosa and daffodils in the arrangements. A cocktail party held on May Day could have the theme of blossom branches and lilies-of-the-valley. The small white flowers of this delicate flower hang down in tiny round bells from pale green stems, and they will be most effective if they are placed in water-filled glass tubes and then inserted into a cone or tree of greenery. Try spraying some lily-of-the-valley cologne around or, if the party is at night, place some lily-of-the-valley perfume on the electric light bulbs so that the heat releases the scent; but do use it sparingly as there is nothing worse than over-scented air.

During the month of May, when tulips abound and lilac comes into bloom, there is nothing more beautiful than arrangements of these flowers massed around the house. Lilac, with its sweet-

Greet your guests with a burst of flowers. Clouds of white gypsophila, interspersed with pink roses and finished off with a pink ribbon, were held in a tall glass spaghetti jar standing on a chest of drawers.

*This tall green vase, standing on a matching base, was ideal for this party arrangement of
flowers and fruit. The fruit was held in place with wooden cocktail sticks.*

*A tall decoration, visible from all over the room, was composed of roses held in wet floral foam
and arranged in a three-tiered stand.*

Your party flower arrangements will be even more effective if you carry through a colour scheme. These lilies, which were held in a tall block of floral foam, were chosen to echo the colours of the furnishings in the room.

are certain to create a greater impact than if vases of various coloured blooms are dotted about the house. I once chose red, using flowers of all tints and shades of this exciting colour. I placed the arrangements around the house and on the serving table. The only relief was given by a frill of apple green ribbon placed around a posy of carnations, which I set on the curled banister at the foot of the stairs, holding it firmly in place with adhesive tape.

For a cocktail party held in mid-summer, all-white with green will create a cool effect. The beauty of white daisies and roses, for example, can be heightened by bowls of green apples, dishes of green olives and cheese-filled celery on a bed of lettuce and by the addition of green candles. The white tablecloth can be criss-crossed with green ribbon, the ends of which can be held down with bunches of greenery pinned to the cloth.

One point to remember is that arrangements for cocktail parties should be placed as high as possible because your guests will be standing most of the time and low arrangements will be obscured from view.

smelling branches of mauve, purple and white blossom, can be used with no other floral additions. But remember to remove all the leaves and allow the split stem ends to stand in deep water overnight. Lilac can be cut short and arranged at the top of a tall candelabra or placed in a low bowl to great effect, especially if the pink, mauve and purple colour scheme is emphasized with pink table cloths and if pink-tinted drinks are served. Purple and mauve flowers tend to appear rather dull and if the party is in the evening, try fixing a spot-light to focus on the lilac as this will help overcome the problem. Pinks show up especially well when artificial light is shone on to them.

Flowers of one colour are sure to be noticed and

ℬUFFETS

Buffet parties are perhaps the most delightful way of entertaining friends and guests. There is a casualness about them that allows the host and hostess, after all their hard work, to relax and enjoy the company of the guests.

The flower arrangements for a buffet table are best if a candelabra or tall-stemmed container is used. This allows the arrangement to be seen from across the room as well as leaving more space on the table for dishes. The arrangement can be placed either in the centre of the table with the drinks at one end and the food at the other, or a tall decoration can be placed at each end of the serving table with the food placed centrally.

Using a single colour is often especially effective at cocktail parties. Here, a round tray, filled with wet floral foam, was placed on a tall stand. A few yellow lilies were inserted into the foam, and the fronds of golden rod (Solidago 'Goldenmosa') were added all around. Using a tall stand such as this leaves room for the food and drink below.

If it is possible to place the buffet table in front of the fireplace, the mantelshelf and the surrounds can be decorated with flowers and trailing foliage. The decorations, whether they are of fruit and flowers or flowers and foliage or simply bright tablecloths with candles placed in wine bottles, will all help to add to the general relaxed atmosphere.

If your setting will allow it, try to include vines or trailing creepers in your decorative scheme. You may even want to combine these with bunches of grapes and a few ears of wheat and barley and bright, informal flowers.

For a more formal occasion at home, there can be nothing more lovely than grapes and vines with a few flowers spilling over from the rims of fine china vases or compote dishes. Candlelight, whether from candles in a candelabra or wine bottles, is ideally suited to the mellow atmosphere of a wine and cheese party.

Many variations are possible for a special buffet party, and different themes can be interpreted with the use of suitable containers and floral material. For instance, if the party food includes a special fish dish, the theme can be emphasized by making use of all the different shapes and colours of shells that are available (see Chapter 3). If you are feeling adventurous, include a fishing net in the main arrangement or drape one around the base of the buffet table!

$\mathcal{F}$ORMAL DINNER PARTIES
❀

The flower arrangements for a dinner party will be affected by several things – the colour of the china and tablecloth you will be using, for example, as well as the size and shape of the table. Unless you have a particular reason for using certain colours, try to select flowers that will echo the colour of the china, the tablecloth or even some dominant furnishing in the room. Many

people, for instance, have paintings or prints on the dining-room walls. If these are of flowers, a charming idea is to copy the flower arrangement depicted in the painting. If possible, try to pick or buy identical blooms; otherwise substitute similar flowers of the same colour. It is always interesting to see how many guests notice the reproduction flower arrangement.

If you are arranging flowers for a large, oblong table, the arrangement will usually be low and be placed in the centre, possibly flanked on each side with tall candlestick arrangements. Tall designs are fine as long as they do not interfere with the guests, who must be able to converse easily across the table. There is nothing more annoying than a flower arrangement that continually gets in the way.

To make a candlestick arrangement, insert a candle cup holder into the top of the candlestick, holding it firmly in place with plasticine or florist's clay. Fill it with floral foam and insert a candle, pressing it down, right through the foam; better still, use a candle holder. The flowers can then be inserted around the base of the candle, with stems of ivy or similar foliage flowing downwards. Candles should be of a matching or contrasting colour. A candelabra can be decorated in the same way, although this will depend on the shape and style of the candelabra. If it has only two candle sockets, place the flowers in the centre, above the supporting column. Again, ivy or other trailing greenery can be used to stretch down and along the centre of the table to join up with the low central arrangement.

Ideally, the container for the low central design should match the candlesticks, but this is not essential as not much of it will be visible. Almost any bowl, or even a vegetable tureen, filled with floral foam can be used. Make the low centrepiece 10–12in. (25–30cm) high and as long as the table will allow. Insert the chosen flowers in a horizontal design, using the choicest possible flowers for special dinner parties – roses, carnations, camellias or lilies, for example.

If space is limited, make a tall arrangement of short-stemmed roses. A stick was passed through the centre of a long block of floral foam so that it would be held securely in the vase, and the roses were inserted into the foam. Lime green Alchemilla mollis *(lady's mantle) was inserted between the roses to hide the foam.*

If your party is going to be a stand-up affair, keep your flower decorations high – on a mantelshelf as here, for example. These summer flowers were held in wet floral foam in a baking tin, and matching circlets were made for the candlesticks.

This attractive centre-piece for an outdoor lunch table was composed of 'Margaret Merril' roses and sprays of white hebe. The brown accessories provided a perfect foil to the white blooms.

This parallel style of table decoration was composed of groups of liatris and larkspur at the ends with pinks and roses lower in the centre, while near the rim came godetias and heads of achillea and a group of 'Pearl' chrysanthemums. Make sure whatever you place low one side is carried through to the other. This gives a growing herbaceous border effect, the stems being inserted up and down into floral foam in a long, plastic plant container.

Ordinary, everyday flowers such as marguerites, scabious and wallflowers, are more suitable for luncheon tables. However, avoid flowers that are heavily scented as this will interfere with the aroma of the foods and wines. Remember, too, that the design will be seen from all sides.

Fruit can be used as an attractive addition to a centre-piece, but make sure that you add the fruit while you are arranging the flowers and allow some of the flowers to protrude from among the fruit. If you add fruit at the end, it will look as if you have added it as an afterthought and it will not form an integral part of the design.

Round tables look best with a round arrangement in the centre. If your table is large enough, you can place four candlesticks symmetrically around the arrangement.

Remember, too, that it is not just the dining table itself that will require decoration. If you have

Plastic candle holders are available from florists and from garden centres. Insert the holder into the pre-soaked floral foam before you add the flowers and foliage.

a sideboard or serving table, this will also require an arrangement.

If originality is your aim, you could try placing three cake-stands, one on top of the other, and filling them with green grapes or hydrangea heads, interspersed with small bunches of violets or gentians. A conversation piece could be created by the depiction of a scene, while some wonderful modern designs can be created from fruit, leaves and driftwood.

One-colour designs can look particularly effective on a contrasting tablecloth, and the colour of the cloth itself can influence the way an arrangement appears – a pink cloth may make an arrangement look dainty, while a yellow cloth will convey a bright, cheerful atmosphere. Green cloths tend to have a refreshing effect, while mauve and écru are suitable for formal occasions. Tablecloths are easy to tint with cold-water dyes, which can be easily washed out, or you may prefer to keep several lengths of nylon in various colours, which you can place over a basic white cloth.

When you plan table arrangements, remember that the relationship of the flowers to the cloth, mats, china, cutlery and glass is important.

CHRISTMAS DECORATIONS

At Christmas time the world glows with loving thoughts. Smiles are exchanged, quarrels are forgotten, presents are given, kind messages are written and an atmosphere of goodwill pervades everything. It is in the home that this atmosphere is more evident than elsewhere, for it is mainly here that family parties – dinners, suppers, cocktail parties and buffet lunches – take place.

The Christmas tree is usually the focal point of all the decorations. If you keep to fresh green and red decorations on the tree, it is a good idea to carry the theme through the house. This includes the use of sprays of evergreen foliage, red ribbons

Opposite: This formal arrangement for a summer dinner table was composed of roses, variegated mint and lavender, and fruit was added to the front and back. The candles gave height to the table setting.

and coloured glass baubles. You might prefer to choose a different colour scheme – pink and silver, red and gold, or turquoise, purple, copper and white, for example – but once you have chosen your colour scheme, repeat it all through your home.

If your Christmas tree is to be displayed near to an open fire, it will be less of a fire hazard if you fireproof it. Mix 2oz (approximately 50g) of ammonia phosphate, which can be obtained from most chemists, with just under 1 gallon (4.5 litres) of water, stand the tree outside on a piece of newspaper and spray or splash it with this solution. Freshly cut or rooted trees will not burn as easily, so it is not as necessary to fireproof them. They should, however, stand in a tub of wet soil or wet, crumpled newspaper. If your tree still has roots, re-cut the dry root ends and add a teaspoonful of fertilizer to the water or soil to help stimulate fresh growth. You can also buy proprietary sprays to help preserve the tree's moisture and to prevent needle drop.

Plan your colour scheme and decorations well in advance and set aside an afternoon for painting and glittering. If you enjoy a gold and glittery effect, lightly spray the tree with gold paint, placing red bows on the branches. Carry through this colour scheme with a decoration for the centre of the table made with gilded leaves, fruit and red candles. Make a hanging decoration by tying a cluster of golden baubles with red ribbon and hanging them from a light pendant.

An effective arrangement can be created by decorating the rim of a small basket with greenery, holly and berries, then filling the basket with gold-painted nuts or with sweets wrapped in gold-coloured foil. Lay these baskets around on small tables. Small 'trees' also look attractive on small tables, and they are especially effective if several round tables are being used for parties. Tie up bunches of greenery with wide red ribbon to hang on the outside door, and leave tall, burning candles in a window with undrawn curtains for all who pass to recognize the glow of goodwill.

Holly and ivy were used in pre-Christian times. They were believed to be plants with magical powers that could ward off evil. The Christian use of holly and ivy for Christmas decorations was probably a continuation of the ancient custom of gathering greenery at the time of the winter solstice. This greenery was used in rituals to ensure that the crops and vegetation returned the following spring.

To prevent church arrangements from appearing too green, include some of the foliage of variegated varieties of holly, aucuba, euonymus and ivy in the arrangements. The ivy *Hedera canariensis* 'Variegata' (also sold as 'Gloire de Marengo') has large leaves with dark green centres, which are surrounded by silver and edged with pale cream, while one of the finest varieties of the common ivy (*Hedera helix*) is the golden-leaved 'Buttercup' (or 'Golden Cloud'). *H. helix* 'Marginata' has a geen-blue centre with a cream edge that has a pink tint in the winter. Flower-bearing ivy can often be found clinging to trees in the country or in the hedgerows, and the domed flowers, which are made up of a mass of round umbels, can be sprayed gold so that they stand out against the shiny green leaves.

Holly, which is usually chosen for its clusters of bright red berries, can also be found with variegated leaves. Look out for the silver-edged leaves of *Ilex aquifolium* 'Argentea Marginata' or 'Ferox Argentea', which has spines of pale cream and which can be used to great effect in an arrangement of mixed foliage. Artificial holly berries can be added to the leaves if necessary.

The Christmas rose (*Helleborus niger*) can, as its name suggests, be found in gardens from December onwards. It has been grown in England since the sixteenth century. An arrangement of these white, saucer-shaped flowers for a chapel or altar arrangement is not only beautiful but appropriate for the setting. Before you arrange the flowers, drag a pin down the stems and leave them in deep water with a little sugar added.

Different shades of green can be brought into

At Christmas time, tables are often too crowded for flower arrangements, and a sideboard decoration can be an ideal way of setting the mood. Here, a candelabra, with festive red candles, was set behind a dish filled with greenery, fruit and brilliant red carnations. The variegated foliage was holly, ivy and Euonymus fortunei *'Silver Queen'.*

Three red glass night-light containers were placed on upturned wine glasses set amid holly and brightly coloured baubles to make a pretty decoration for a side-table.

the church by including stems or branches of hemlock, yew, spruce or pine. Many of these may still have cones on them, which will look particularly attractive if they are flicked with white paint or artificial snow. It is advisable to wire the cones in place as they have a tendency to fall when they are brought into a warm environment. The foliage of evergreens such as Mexican orange (*Choisya ternata*), spotted laurel (*Aucuba japonica*), *Skimmia japonica* and laurustinus (*Viburnum tinus*) is also very useful.

As always, before deciding on the Christmas designs, you must take the interior of the church into account. Think carefully before using gold- or silver-painted foliage, as this will be lost if the church has ornately painted screens or an intricately carved reredos. The natural beauty of the foliage and flowers will not be lost even if they are left unadorned. Many old churches have beautiful candle sconces, and greenery, flowers

and red ribbon can be hung from these.

Pedestal arrangements (see Chapter 6) will look magnificent standing either side of the chancel steps. Use variegated holly with pale yellow-edged leaves, white or yellow chrysanthemums, trails of ivy and green holly with masses of red berries. The red of the holly berries will complement the greens of the arrangement and accentuate the yellow edges of the variegated leaves.

If the interior of the church is reasonably warm, pots of poinsettia (*Euphorbia pulcherrima*, commonly known as the Christmas flower), can be arranged around the base of the pulpit, the bright green leaves and scarlet bracts will fit in well with the other Christmas arrangements.

No matter how you decorate your home or church, enter into the procedure with care and love, remembering not only the meaning of the day but also the goodwill the whole celebration engenders.

This pendant decoration was made from a large sphere of floral foam into which were inserted short lengths of yew and pine. The arrangement was finished off with red ribbon.

Small 'trees' such as this are perfect decorations for low and individual tables. Place a small sphere of floral foam on a stick, which can be inserted into a plaster- or cement-filled plant pot. (Remember to cover the hole in the base of the plant pot before you add the plaster mix.) Cover the surface of the sphere with short-stemmed dried flowers, leaves and grasses, stand the pot in a container and disguise the surface of the plaster or cement with moss. Tie a length of ribbon into a bow.

A basket edged with the leaves of variegated holly and sprigs of pine and filled with bright red baubles and nuts was an ideal decoration for a coffee-table. It was finished off with a bright red bow.

A hanging arrangement is an ideal way of decorating a small area between two rooms. Take a wide length of felt or ribbon, and use a darning needle and strong thread or fine string to sew on sprigs of foliage and artificial fruit. A decoration of this kind will last well into the New Year.

Opposite: A plastic ring was filled with floral foam into which were inserted short stems of variegated holly and cupressus. Clementines on wooden sticks and baubles were added to complete the arrangement.

WEDDING RECEPTIONS

The style of arrangement will largely depend where the reception is held; this may be in a hotel, a marquee, a hall or in the bride's home. However, do make sure that some of the flowers are placed as high as possible.

A large pedestal group before which the bride and groom might stand to receive the guests can be made following the directions for a church group (see Chapter 6). If the reception is a stand-up affair, try to place the arrangements on mantelpieces, wall sconces or any piece of furniture that will provide height. You can make the arrangements for the reception more colourful than those for the wedding itself, but they must suit the surroundings. In a marquee, for example, which is often made of canvas, brighter or more vivid colours might be a better choice. Some marquees are lined with yellow or pink material, others have striped interiors, but whatever the background, try to complement the surroundings with your flowers. Hanging decorations in a marquee are an ideal choice, or you could twine creepers mixed with flowers around the tent poles. To make a hanging decoration you can use a ball or sphere of floral foam covered with thin plastic into which the flowers can be inserted; alternatively, you could use a nurseryman's wire basket lined with plastic film and filled with wet floral foam, which will hold the flowers, some pointing upwards, others flowing downwards. Short-stemmed leaves placed between the flowers will cover the wire basket.

Make tall arrangements to stand at each end of the food and drinks table by decorating a candelabra that is standing on a draped box, or make a conically shaped arrangement.

Should the guests be seated at individual tables, you might like to try making small flower 'trees' one for each table or you could surround a candle (unlit) with flowers standing in a saucer-like bowl of floral foam.

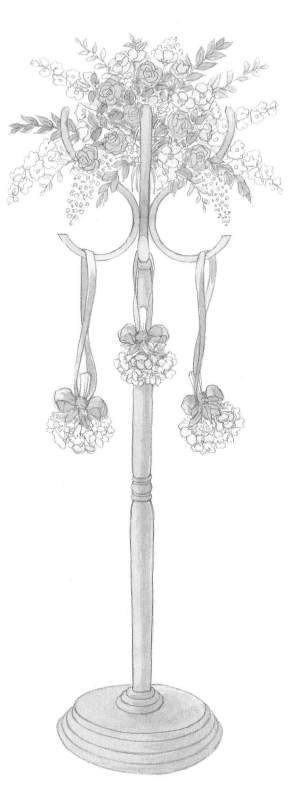

A pretty idea for a wedding reception is to hang the little spheres of flowers that the bridesmaids have carried on a hatstand, which can be decorated with a larger arrangement made of similar flowers.

*A large arrangement of pale colours is ideal for a wedding reception. Here sprays of
Philadelphus (mock orange), pink peonies and white campanulas are held firmly in a large
cache-pot filled with crumpled wire netting. Make sure the flowers flow forwards over the rim of
the vase.*

The wedding is over. The lilies, bridesmaid's headdress and shawl are laid on a low side-table while the celebrations continue elsewhere.

WEDDING ANNIVERSARIES

Wedding anniversaries call for a celebration, and the main ones, such as silver and gold, are often marked with a party. It is a thoughtful and pleasant idea to introduce, with floral decorations, some of the symbols that are attached to these anniversaries.

A silver wedding, which celebrates 25 years of marriage, should have flower arrangements that introduce silver. This can be done by arranging white flowers in a silver bowl or vase with a silver ribbon or tinsel. If you do not have a silver vase, use a grey pottery vase or use spray paint to coat a vase or tin with silver. It is in these silver arrangements that good use can be made of the beautiful foliage of silver-leaved shrubs and plants. *Artemisia arborescens* (wormwood) has silver-white leaves and *Senecio maritimus* shows the whitest leaves in the garden, 'Silver Dust' and 'Diamond' being the two best varieties. Lamb's tongue (*Stachys byzantina* syn. *S. lanata*) is very popular in cottage gardens, and the variety 'Silver Carpet' is especially good when foliage is required as it does not produce flowers. Lavender grows in most gardens, and its slender blue flowering spikes fit in well with silver flower arrangements. White roses are a fitting flower to arrange among the silver foliage. 'Iceberg', a floribunda rose, which is perfect in form and is also fragrant, is an ideal choice. Table decorations can incorporate white or silver candles, and silver doilies can be placed under arrangements or used as place mats.

A golden wedding celebration is very special and here gold-coloured flowers should feature. There are so many to choose from in this colour range – chrysanthemums, roses, gerberas, carnations, dahlias, gladioli and day lilies to name just a few. It

is a charming gesture if the main flower arrangement is designed from the same flowers as the bride carried on her wedding day. These could be arranged in a golden-coloured vase or, if possible, in a vase or bowl that was an original wedding present. Alternatively, any existing vase or basket can easily be sprayed or painted gold.

The table covering can be gold lamé or gauze, and candles, with the number 50 marked on them in gold, can be placed in the centre of the table. Celebrate with a cake, bound in a gold frill, and use gold paper doilies. The number 50 should be a prominent feature, and the figures can be cut out of cardboard and covered with gold paper or painted gold. The celebration drink should, of course, be sparkling wine or champagne.

It is not only the main wedding anniversaries that can be celebrated with flowers. The symbols traditionally used to describe many of the other wedding anniversaries can be interpreted however you like, and they offer a wide choice to stimulate the flower arranger's imagination. They would probably make an interesting subject for a competition.

Some of the most successful parties I have attended or given have been planned around the flowers, and wedding anniversaries are ideal opportunites to use flowers to make the day doubly memorable. Food and drink are very important, of course, but guests will often remember long after the event that 'burst of yellow and white flowers' or that 'large pedestal group of red flowers spot-lit from above'. Remember to use the colour of the main arrangements at other strategic points – in a hall or on the dining-table for instance. You could even place posies in small tins or jars up the stairs (as long as they are wide enough) to add to the general impact of colour. So let your flowers speak.

This blue and white group greeted the guests at a wedding reception held at home. White gladioli and blue larkspur were used to give height and width, white stocks were used to fill out the base of the arrangement and blue Agapanthus was used in the centre, and white blooms of Lilium longiflorum were inserted here and there. White carnations were added around the base of the arrangement. All the stems were held in a large cache-pot filled with water-soaked floral foam, which was taped into the pot to give additional stability.

Artificial silver leaves and white roses make this attractive silver wedding arrangement. Cover the water-soaked floral foam with kitchen foil and place in a silver dish or container. Insert the longest pointed leaves for the outline, with some pointing forward, and place the roses in between. Silver wedding presents can be placed as a display on a side-table.

Main Wedding Anniversaries

1st – Cotton	10th – Tin
2nd – Paper	15th – Crystal
3rd – Leather	20th – China
4th – Fruit and flowers	25th – Silver
5th – Wooden	30th – Pearl
6th – Sugar	35th – Coral
7th – Woollen	40th – Ruby
8th – Salt	50th – Golden
9th – Copper	60th – Diamond

Candles and Flowers

Candles are nowadays made in every conceivable size, shape and colour. You can buy small, squat, straight-sided ones or tall, elegant, barley-sugar twists. Few combinations associate as well as flowers and candles: tall candles can be used to give height to a low grouping of flowers, while coloured candles can be used to add contrast to, or harmonize with, almost any decoration, whether they are lit or not. The glow that lighted candles produce adds a touch of intimacy, which other lighting seems to disperse, and for this reason, in winter, when flowers are expensive and scarce, a few candles are welcome additions to any type of table decoration.

Grouped together in various colours with just a few flowers added, they can make exciting and unusual accessories. For a decoration for a rustic setting, for example, try placing candles in shades of cream, tan and brown into a block of wet floral foam or use a candle holder. If you do not have a candle holder, use adhesive tape to bind four cocktail sticks or hairpins to the base of the candle and then insert these prongs into the floral foam to hold the candle firmly upright. Add a few flame-red chrysanthemums and some autumn foliage around the base to conceal the foam. The candles will provide the necessary height, and you will need only a handful of flowers to complete the arrangement. You could place the composition on a wooden base or in a wooden bowl together with a few nuts to make an even more effective composition.

Driftwood can provide an unusual but complementary texture when it is used with candles, although I do feel that it should be kept for rustic settings. You could, for example, place a group of white candles in a tray of sand and add some shells and pieces of driftwood to give a seaside effect.

I once made an all-green design with lime, apple, bottle and olive green candles of different heights with pale green grapes and shiny green peppers and apples. I thought it looked stunning!

A selection of candles in pale pink, deep pink, crimson and cerise will look most effective when grouped with pink crysanthemums and anemones as a table decoration. For a party or special occasion you might like to combine brilliant turquoise-blue, chunky candles with silver-painted leaves. One of the simplest table decorations to make is to stand a thick green candle on a block of wet floral foam, which should be placed on a cake-stand. Insert some short-stemmed flower heads – yellow single chrysanthemums, for instance – into the foam to make the candle appear to be standing in a ring of flowers. This type of arrangement needs only two stems of spray chrysanthemums, which is a great saving at the time of year when flowers are expensive.

If you are fond of pressed flowers, you can use them to decorate the sides of candles, either by gluing tiny pieces of fern or flat, dry petals to the candle or by piercing them through the centres with a hot pin. When they are in position, paint over the flower heads with hot, clear candle wax or clear varnish. Flower-covered candles make delightful and very personal gifts. In Mexico candles are decorated most beautifully with dried flowers. Pink flowers on purple candles or purple flowers on pink candles look exceptionally attractive, and I once glued a few pink sequins to some candles I was using with some anemones. I have also cut out the

An elderly member of the family had specifically requested that violets be used at a party held in her honour. The glass candle-sticks were filled with water to which a few spots of purple ink had been added. Purple candles completed the scheme, and echoed the colour of the violets in a glass dish on a mauve-coloured base.

'flower heads' from a length of lace I had bought from a haberdashers and glued them to some green candles rising from a low bed of marguerites.

I love chunky candles and often give them as Christmas presents. Square candles – sold as Gem lights – are available, and these are sometimes covered in glitter, which makes them especially suitable for Christmas and other festive occasions. You could also use a thin, non-flammable glue to write someone's name or the words 'Christmas' or 'Happy Birthday' along the candle and then sprinkle the letters with diamanté glitter.

Candles placed in the neck of a wine bottle can be made to look more decorative if they are encircled with flowers or foliage. Place a thick ring of plasticine (modelling clay) around the neck of the bottle and push sprigs of greenery and berries into it. You can also mix some artificial flowers in with the natural foliage. If the candles are too thick for the top of the wine bottle or candlestick, dip the ends in hot water for a minute or two to soften the wax so that you can press them into place.

When you extinguish candles you can avoid spilling the hot wax if you place your forefinger close to your lips, horizontally, and blow across it. And bear in mind that candles will burn down more slowly if they are kept in a refrigerator before use.

CHAPTER SIX

Flowers for the Church

Very little has been written on the true role of flowers in churches, and although we know that many centuries ago monks grew flowers to place on the altars of the monasteries, today, as flower arranging becomes ever more popular, they are being used frequently as expressions of love and adornment as well as for special events such as weddings, festivals, christenings, harvest and Easter.

So, although flowers can play an important part in our lives at home, it is in church that they take on a special significance. There are a number of factors to consider when you are asked to arrange flowers in a church. You should study the style of the building and its architecture and plan the arrangements to suit the settings, making sure that you enhance and do not overpower them. To obtain the best effect from your flowers, try to study the various places within the church that might be brought into play. Of course, if you are a member of the flower arranging rota in your local church you will be familiar with the preferences of the vicar, and the places where flowers can be placed. However, if you are doing the flowers for a family wedding, for example, it is as well to plan an early visit to familiarize yourself with the size of the arrangement you may be required to make. You should also find out whether the bride would like flowers in the porch, on the window-sills or pew ends or as a hanging decoration.

Flowers that are placed in front of stained-glass windows should blend in with the colours of the windows. A church with clear windows and slim columns will require delicate, graceful arrangements, while a dark, wood-panelled church needs light colours, such as white, pale pink or yellow, to bring light into the church. A pale background will not show up pale-hued flowers, and an outline of dark foliage, such as camellia or beech, would be a good choice as a dark background to throw lighter coloured flowers into prominence.

Preserved foliage is always a useful stand-by as a background, especially where you are limited by the amount of money you can spend on the arrangement (see Chapter 9).

Having studied the design of the church, it is also important to study the district in which the church lies, for this will often help you to decide the type of flowers to be used. For instance, a very modern church in a comparatively new community can take flowers with bold, strong lines, such as gladioli or arum lilies, incorporated with bare branches. A more ornately styled church in a settled town will demand richer flowers with more flowing lines. A country church arrangement of sophisticated flowers, such as carnations or anthuriums, would be quite out of place when the surrounding area abounds with wild and cottage garden flowers.

This mahogany candle holder was surrounded with bunches of gypsophila held in water-soaked floral foam.

A garland of short flowers was attached to the balustrade with florist's tape and finished off with a round bowl of pink and white flowers. Similar flowers were made for the other side, both leading to the altar.

If you are arranging flowers in your local church you will already know the clergyman. If you are in a strange church you must make yourself known and explain what you wish to do and where you would like the arrangements to stand. Some clergy have fixed ideas about where the flowers should be placed. He will also show you where any rubbish may be put and where the church containers are kept.

Some churches have a good collection of containers, others have only a few, and it is here you can help (with permission) by providing some vases yourself. It is also easier to arrange flowers in your own familiar containers. A useful container, and one that can be found in almost all homes, is a baking tin, providing it is watertight (two coats of varnish will help). This can be painted and weighted by placing some gravel in the bottom; when this is filled with crumpled wire netting it becomes a very useful container for the window-sill.

It is important to find out when it is convenient for you to work in the church. Some churches are kept locked unless they are being used for a service, so you will have to find out where the key is kept. Most church flowers are changed on a Friday or Saturday morning so that they are at their best for the Sunday worship.

Whether you are a member of a team working together in a large church or cathedral, or taking your turn on a rota system, the equipment you will need to take with you is the same. You should have a watering can with a long thin spout (for topping up the finished arrangement), containers, wire netting, wire cutters, floral foam, pin-holders, florist's scissors, a sharp knife, string, wire, secateurs and a bucket. You should also always use a large sheet of polythene to protect the floor and surface you are working on, because all flowers should be arranged where they are to stand. You can spread your flowers and foliage on the sheet so that it is easy to select the material you need. Lay the blooms and foliage in groups of tall, medium and short.

PEDESTAL ARRANGEMENTS

Many churches possess pedestals made from wood, stone, wrought-iron, gilt or brass, and these are ideal for arrangements as they are tall and allow the flowers to be seen easily from most parts

Fill the container with pre-soaked floral foam, using several pieces if necessary. You may also wish to press the floral foam on to a pin-holder to give extra stability. Cover the foam and container with wire netting and fasten the whole thing to the pedestal with tape or string. Then position the tallest stems that are to form the outline of the arrangement.

This pedestal arrangement of spring flowers would be suitable for an Easter service or a spring wedding. The twisty stems of forsythia created the framework, and lilies were used as the central point of interest. Daffodils and other spring flowers were used to fill in. Note how the flowers flow forwards over the rim and unite with the trails of ivy and periwinkle foliage.

of the church. A pedestal should be solid and stand firmly on the ground. It should also be capable of supporting a heavy arrangement. There is not always a matching vase for the pedestal, but any vase, bowl or even a large cake tin will do for an arrangement where the flowers and foliage will conceal the container, as long as it is not too deep and has a flat base so that it will fit squarely and safely on the pedestal. An urn-shaped vase is ideal when the container is intended to be visible. Place gravel or small stones in the bottom of the vase to make it more stable.

When two pedestals are to be used, perhaps to be placed either side of the chancel steps, there is a problem of producing two identical flower arrangements. It is best to divide the flowers into two matching groups before you start the arrangement. Fill the vase with crumpled wire netting, making sure it reaches over and above the rim. Some arrangers can manage with only wire netting in the bowl, but I prefer to place a pin-holder underneath the wire to help hold the first and tallest stems firmly in place. Other arrangers press floral foam on to the pin-holder and then cover it with wire netting. Tie the whole thing, bowl as well, to the pedestal to keep it firm. It is best to use string, because wire may damage the pedestal. Having placed the bowl on the pedestal, fill it almost to the rim with water; this will stop the stems from drying out while you arrange the flowers and so help them to last longer. The vase can be topped up with water from the back when the arrangement is complete.

I am often asked which flowers to choose and this, of course, depends upon whether you are buying from a florist or picking the flowers from the garden. The season of the year also determines the type of flowers available. In all cases though, try to pick some fine tall leaves or flowers for the outline, such as gladioli, Michaelmas daisies (asters), eremurus (foxtail lily), delphiniums and the pointed leaves of iris. Include some large flowers for the centre and some medium ones for filling in. Avoid blue flowers if the background is stone, because these will not be seen from a distance. Try to pick some trailing ivy or other leaves to swerve down over the rim of the container, which will help unite the vase to the pedestal.

Having decided whether you are going to use light or dark flowers and leaves, start by making a triangular pattern with the tallest and most pointed flowers. Aim for height at the centre. Some people find when making these large arrangements that the flowers overbalance and fall backwards or forwards. This should not happen if your first stem is placed centrally and two-thirds back in the vase. If your arrangement is inclined to topple forwards, this can be corrected by hanging a weight from the wire at the back of the vase. A piece of lead or a spare pin-holder is ideal for this. Another good tip is to insert some stems flowing out at the back to balance those you place pointing forward.

After establishing the height and width with the pointed flowers, strengthen the centre line with bigger, bolder or rounder flowers. Then add some leaves low down near to the centre and finally fill in with medium flowers, working from the outside of the design to the centre, aiming all the stems to a point beneath the tallest central stems. Make sure that some of the low flowers or leaves flow forwards over the rim of the vase, allowing them to protrude. This will stop the flower arrangement looking flat. Add some shorter stems at the back, again to avoid the appearance of a flat-backed arrangement. There should always be plenty of space between the flowers in a large arrangement so that they can be seen by all the congregation. If small, closely packed flowers are used, the effect from the back of the church will be just a blob and the beauty of the blooms will be lost. This idea of using, first, tall and thin material for the outline or pattern, then bigger more important flowers in the centre and, finally, filling in with medium flowers can be followed whether you are making large or small arrangements.

Dahlias from the garden were combined with white larkspur and pale lemon shaggy chrysanthemums in this autumn pedestal arrangement. The tassel-like flowers of Amaranthus caudatus 'Viridis' (love-lies-bleeding) were placed in the centre, and variegated foliage was used to flow forward. Place heavy foliage at the back to avoid the arrangement toppling forward.

Sprays of pink and white larkspur were combined with
roses and the silvery-grey foliage of Artemisia
absinthium 'Lambrook Silver' to form the outline of this
decoration, which was hung over the entrance to a
church. An oblong block of wet floral foam held in a wire
cage was used to keep the flowers in place.

WEDDING FLOWERS

The growing interest in flower arranging means that you may be asked to help with the flowers at a family wedding. Think carefully before you take on this task, for although it can prove both enjoyable and rewarding, it can also be a tiring experience. It might be as well to obtain the help of friends, even if they only obtain the water for you or clear up the rubbish.

The pedestal group of flowers is the most popular for this occasion because of the height which can be obtained. Even more height can be obtained by using cones, so follow the directions for making a pedestal group, given earlier in this chapter.

Sometimes tall, vertical stands filled with flowers are used each side of the altar, at other times a floor-standing group can be created. However, in this latter case, do remember that although the bridal group and those in the first two or three rows will be able to appreciate these flowers, those sitting further back will be able to see only the top.

The style you decide upon and the colour scheme will, of course, be the choice of the bride, so an early visit to the church with the bride will help make those decisions.

White is a traditional colour scheme for weddings and white flowers look particularly lovely when they are combined with fresh green leaves. White gladioli, larkspur or delphiniums are ideal for the framework, while white lilies centrally placed, with roses in between and carnations flowing down at the sides will make a very beautiful group. Branches of lime flowers, stripped of their dark green leaves, also make an ideal background for white lilies and roses, and although the bride may want to include some colour to complement the bridesmaids' dresses or even some colour of her choice, do advise her against including blue, for this colour will fade

into a dark grey or black when seen from a distance in the interior of a church. Of course, you can overcome this by using a spot-light, but in my opinion it is far better to incorporate yellow, cream, peach or pink flowers into the arrangement.

Soak the floral foam holder for 30 minutes and leave to drain. You can insert fine stems or greenery on the outside of the block, longer stems at the base and shorter ones at the top. Fill in with larger flowers or fruit, adding pointed stems in between. Finally, tie ribbon to the pew end.

If there is a particular variety that the bride wishes to have in the church, it is wise to check with your florist or the market to see if it will be available at the time. Most florists can order flowers that they do not normally carry in stock, but if this is not possible they can usually suggest a good alternative in colour or shape. Availability will depend very much on the time of the year, but whatever flowers are selected, remember to place your order well in advance of the wedding. Gladioli, lilies and some peonies come on to the market in very tight bud and can take three or more days to open fully. So be warned.

Wedding flowers are best arranged the day before the ceremony, so that the arrangement can settle overnight. The flowers can then be checked the following morning, the containers topped up with water and any necessary repairs carried out. It is always advisable to keep a few flowers in reserve for this purpose.

If you are including window-sill arrangements, decorating pew ends, placing flowers in the porch or making a hanging decoration, it is wise to prepare all your mechanics the day before – otherwise, if you are a guest at the wedding, you will be too exhausted to enjoy the reception.

When I was researching for my book *Flowers in Praise* I visited a famous church where I noticed two beautiful urns filled with various kinds of leaves at the entrance. Inside, two pedestals were also filled with similar leaves, and I thought the idea was very original. I later discovered that the arranger had prepared everything in advance – inserting all the mechanics and foliage – so that all she had to do the next morning was to add the flowers. So give yourself time to prepare your containers. Fill them with crumpled wire netting or floral foam well in advance and tie them down firmly to the pedestal or window-sill or wherever they are to be positioned, for nothing is more disconcerting than watching flowers move or even fall over in the middle of the service.

At the same time, do please leave the making of bouquets for the bride and bridesmaids to your florist. This is a professional job requiring long training, and the amateur should not attempt it, even with the aid of a posy holder. The professional knows from experience how to wire and tie every stem firmly in place. Stems might fall out of a bouquet made by a family friend or the wire might stab the hand of the bride or tear her dress.

CHRISTENINGS

Flower arrangements for a christening service should be kept very simple and should be confined to the font and the area surrounding it. The word 'font' is derived from the Latin word for 'stream' and it dates back to when the baptism ceremony called for total immersion in water. Fonts are usually situated near the main church entrance, and they vary in size, style and structure depending on the age or architecture of the church.

If there is a window-sill or ledge near the font, this could be decorated too, to enhance the joy of the occasion, but if the font itself is to be decorated, especially round the top of the rim, try to leave space for the clergyman's arm to reach the holy water. A thick, plastic, sausage-like roll filled with wet floral foam can be fixed round the top of the rim with florist's tape or adhesive tape. If it proves difficult to insert delicate flowers, such as snowdrops, scillas and primroses, into the plastic, try tying a few stems to a cocktail stick with wool and inserting them as a bunch through the plastic. Bows of ribbon can also be inserted where the ends meet. I have also used small shallow tins filled with wet floral foam; these I placed around the top of the rim, holding them firmly in place by taping them to the rim and then filling them with dainty flowers and foliage. Flowers can also be placed round the base of the font, so leaving the rim completely free, or a long thin group, again held down firmly with tape, can be placed on one side of the rim.

The flowers at a christening reception can be arranged in a similar fashion to those at a wedding reception (see Chapter 5), although it is a good idea to carry through the blue or pink motif with ribbons, napkins and other accessories. A charming idea is to present each guest with a net bag of sugared almonds tied with ribbon in the appropriate colour or, though more expensive, with a small china trinket embossed with the name of the child. Bowls of sugar almonds placed around on tables will, with the flowers, help to make the occasion a memorable one.

HARVEST FESTIVALS

The Christian church celebrates harvest festival with a thanksgiving service during which local people bring gifts of harvest fare into the church. Flower arrangements should, therefore, be kept to a minimum so that they do not detract from the main harvest display.

Your floral arrangements will be more in keeping with the occasion if they are limited to the russet colours of autumn, so you should make good use of the red, gold and tawny coloured leaves that can be found in most gardens and woods at this time of year. Stalks of bearded wheat are always appreciated in town churches. Wheat

Garlands can be made by inserting blocks of pre-soaked floral foam into garland cages, as shown in the drawing. These are a new idea – the units can be linked together and built up to the required length. There is quite a lot of free play between the units to allow you to vary the steepness of the curve. Alternatively, put the pre-soaked floral foam into tubes of thin plastic sheeting. Use string or wool to separate the blocks so that the sausage-like links of foam can be wound around pillars or the base of the font. Use a fine knitting needle to make holes in the plastic so that you can insert the flower stems easily into the foam.

Flowers and fruit were used to create this decoration for a harvest festival party. A circular hole was cut in the top of the melon, and a small dish (a tin would do just as well) containing floral foam was inserted into it. The candle and flowers were held in the foam, and fruit was arranged around the base of the melon.

can be bought from some florists, but if it is not available, it can – with the farmer's permission, of course – be cut from the edges of fields before the combine harvesters set to work. It should then be hung up to dry in a warm, dark place.

There is a wealth of brightly coloured berries available at this time of year, including the orange and red berries of berberis, cotoneaster and pyracantha – or firethorn, as it is aptly named with its long, sharp thorns (wear strong gloves when you cut stems from this shrub). Rose hips can also be successfully incorporated into harvest designs, as can stalks bearing the dried, paper-like orange seedheads of Chinese lanterns (*Physalis alkekengi*, also sometimes called bladder cherry). There are also, of course, the traditional autumn flowers – chrysanthemums, dahlias and gaillardias (blanket flowers) – whose glowing colours blend perfectly with fruit, vegetables and autumn foliage.

At this time of year the hedgerows offer a wealth of foliage and plant material, and the grey-white, fluffy seedheads on long, trailing stalks of old man's beard (*Clematis vitalba*, wild clematis) can be twined around pillars and statues or used in any arrangement that requires hanging lengths of floral material to unite groups of fruits or vegetables. If you spray seedheads gathered from the hedgerow or your own garden with hair lacquer or clear varnish they will not drop their seeds.

Fruit and vegetables do not simply have to be part of the main harvest display; they can be combined with flowers and foliage in large pedestal or tall, cone-shaped designs. Gifts of fruit and vegetables can be placed on the ground around these tall arrangements, but it is advisable if someone with some knowledge of flower arranging is in charge to group them, because many people bring their offerings and just leave them on the floor. Some of the heavier fruits – bunches of grapes, melons, apples and pears, for example – can be placed in low groups. Take care when you use fruits such as black grapes or cherries because they can leave nasty stains on altar cloths or other fabric coverings in the church. It is best to place them on plastic or paper plates.

Ornamental gourds, pumpkins and squashes, grown from seed sown earlier in the year, come in all shapes and sizes: some have smooth skins, others knobbly, wart-like ones, and the colours range from green through to orange, yellow and cream. Pick them when they are completely ripe and their skins are hard, and leave them to dry in an airing cupboard or another warm, dry place until they are needed. Remember to wipe them with a dry cloth from time to time to remove any moisture. The 'Turk's Head' gourd, with its silver stripes on a dark green skin, the round, pale yellow 'Butternut' and the bright orange 'Golden Nugget' are just a few of the many varieties now available. If they are not going to be eaten, you can intensify their colours by painting them with a coat of clear varnish.

Harvest arrangements look their best if the colour of the container harmonizes with the overall colour scheme of the plant material. Copper vases and jugs are perfect, since they reflect the rich colours of the autumnal foliage. Wooden vases and woven baskets are also appropriate, their neutral brown and straw colours blending in with the harvest theme, and you could also use glazed pottery, earthenware, brass, pewter or stone containers. If you can find a farmer who will lend you a milk churn, it is possible to reverse the lid and conceal a bowl inside it. This could be used for a tall arrangement, which would be suitable for near the entrance or at the back of the church. Vegetables could then be arranged around the base.

Swags can be attached to the ends of the first two pews or fastened around pillars or columns. There are no set rules about the type of material that can be used to make a swag; your selection will depend very much on what is available and your own preferences. Dried materials of all kinds lend themselves particularly well to swags, and these can be prepared well in advance of the

Pew-end decorations can be made very simply, but this one was made more ornate for a harvest festival.

Seed heads, leaves, flowers and fruit were arranged in a long loaf tin filled with wet floral foam that fitted on a church window ledge for a harvest festival. Add more fruit, and vegetables and bread to finish the effect.

harvest festival service itself so that you have time to concentrate on the arrangement of the fresh flowers and foliage. To make a swag you will need a mixed collection of dried leaves, flowers, nuts, gourds and cereals. Choose large, flat leaves so that they form a background for other materials; the glorious dark, burnished leaves of copper beech are perfect. The brown and sepia-coloured cones of pine trees, which can be elongated or thick and short, and the elliptical or cylindrical cones of spruce trees are suitable for incorporating into swags, and ripened ornamental maize (sweet corn) can be bought from shops that sell dried flowers and grasses. The variety 'Strawberry Corn' is spherical and has deep red kernels, while *Zea mays* 'Japonica' has tinges of pink and red in its otherwise pale yellow kernels. Peanuts and chestnuts, which are easier to wire than some of the other hard-shelled nuts, will add dashes of beige-brown to the arrangement.

You will have to make a base on which the swag can be built. You will need a piece of wood, 2×¾in. (5×2cm), nine 2½in. (6cm) nails, three polythene-covered blocks of floral foam and some wire netting. Position the nails in groups of three, spacing the groups at even distances, and hammer them through the wood so that the points protrude at one side. Press the polythene-covered blocks of foam onto the nails and wrap wire netting around them to hold them firmly to the wood and nails. The dried material can then be inserted into the foam. Keep the main weight of material in the middle and top blocks, and use the large, flat leaves as a background so that the polythene is completely hidden.

The finished swag can be tied or wired into position or hung on a nail if there is one already in the church. *Never* hammer your own nails into the fabric of the building.

Vegetables not only make effective decorations grouped together or incorporated into arrangements with other floral material, but they can also be used as unusual containers. Pumpkins are ideal for this; use the large, pale orange, globe-shaped pumpkins for large arrangements and the smaller, bell-shaped ones for smaller designs on side-tables.

To use a pumpkin as a container, slice off the top and scoop out the soft flesh inside. Line the hole with kitchen foil or polythene and fill it with water-soaked floral foam. You can then arrange flowers and foliage into this. Branches of brown leaves, sprays of copper and bronze chrysanthemums and dark green foliage, arranged in a pumpkin will make an unusual arrangement for a window-sill. You could also include berried-branches in the design, and the shiny black berries of the evergreen privet (*Ligustrum ovalifolium*) look especially attractive contrasting with the orange skin of a pumpkin. Try to arrange some of the stalks so that clusters of berries hang down over the edge of the container and remember to split the bottom of the stems of woody-stemmed flowers and shrubs before you arrange them.

Whether your arrangements are symmetrical will largely depend on their position, but arrangements incorporating flowers, fruit berries and vegetables need not be formal. When I prepared an arrangement for a window-sill, for example, I used a long loaf tin, which I filled with water-soaked floral foam pressed over two large pin-holders for extra stability. I used branches of larch to give height, and inserted preserved beech leaves (see Chapter 9), seedheads and ears of wheat into the floral foam making sure that I had sufficient berries, dried flowers and leaves to insert around the edge of the foam to flow down over the edge and hide the tin. I added some bronze-coloured chrysanthemums in the centre, and then extended the overall arrangement by adding a loaf of bread, vegetables, berries and cones along the window-sill.

Most of the gifts that are brought into the church for the harvest festival are later distributed to the elderly within the parish or to local hospitals, but whether we celebrate in church or at home, this is an occasion when we who have should give silent thanks and remember those who are not so fortunate.

Branches of blossom were used for this Easter arrangement held by wire-netting in a large bowl.
Make sure branches or leaves flow backwards as well as forwards to avoid the whole arrangement
toppling over. Add water.

CHAPTER SEVEN

Festivals and Flower Shows

FESTIVALS

If you are known to be a flower arranger, whether you do it in your home for your own pleasure or whether you are a member of a flower club, you may find that you are called upon to help with charitable events, which might be staged in settings to which you are un-accustomed. If such an invitation comes your way, seize it, for in working with others, some-times in historic and famous settings, much can be learned.

The fascination of studying colour schemes that assort well with unfamiliar backgrounds and the study of paintings and furniture that is often necessary when designing flowers for historic settings are further extensions of the art of flower arranging. I will never forget the great, shallow pottery bowls, about 4ft (1.2m) wide, filled with branches of azalea, that stood on the top of the tall, floodlit pillars in Ghent Cathedral, Belgium, during the Floralies. Another unforgettable sight was of the massed orchid designs I saw in the Frick Collection in New York.

Flower arrangers have been called upon to assist on many grand occasions. I recall the splendid sight of the flower arrangements in the Hôtel de Ville in Paris during the Third World Flower Arrangement Show, and probably one of the most artistic designs yet seen was the centre-piece, a copy of an antique print, staged in the magnificent Palazzo Spinola, now the Genoese National Gallery, in Italy.

Some years ago, together with other members of the Garden Club, I responded to an invitation to design a flower arrangement incorporating a museum piece in the Metropolitan Museum, New York. We were allowed to place the flowers around or at the base of any item of our choice in the Museum, as long as the flowers were in keeping with the colour and history of the artefact. The festival was staged to encourage the public to visit the Museum, an idea that might usefully be copied in other countries.

Museums, stately homes, historic churches and even European châteaux are all being brought into play as the settings for charitable events. The UK is blessed with thousands of historic churches and cathedrals, which are constantly used as settings for events to raise funds for the restoration of the buildings' fabric. The UK is also fortunate in the large number of stately homes that are still lived in by the descendants of the original families who built them generations ago. These magnificent back-drops offer flower arrangers opportunities to

A special occasion in a special setting calls for the best possible flowers. The chosen colour scheme was pink and gold, and the delicate blooms were backed by sprigs of maroon Berberis thunbergii var. atropurpurea. The bowl was filled with floral foam covered with chicken wire to hold the stems in position.

create designs in a different style and with a wider choice of flowers than are normally available.

It is on occasions such as this that a sound knowledge of the basic mechanics that hold flowers firmly in place becomes important. The arranger has to forget the favourite vase that is used at home or the small niche that is available at a flower show. Now you must think on a large scale and use larger containers than you are used to.

Included in this chapter are illustrations of a few flower arrangements created for charities, and these can be modified for use in other locations and for other purposes. Advanced arrangers may already be practised in making the larger designs required on such occasions, but if you have never done so before, do try to take part in these events in any capacity you can. You will be able to gain experience, not only perhaps of working on a large arrangement yourself, but also of watching more experienced designers creating some of the larger effects.

ℱLOWERS FOR SHOWS
❀

Tens of thousands of people visit flower shows every year, and every year the flower tents and halls offer more and more exciting exhibits, which inspire the enthusiasts to open their eyes to what is around them in the plant world. At the same time, other visitors to the flower tents, seeing an unusual exhibit some 4ft (1.2m) tall, will remark that 'It all depends on whether you have that structure' or 'I could never have that at home'.

Flower festivals are often staged in aid of charities in stately homes. Here, in Goodwood House, Sussex, I used forsythia to create the overall triangular shape, adding daffodils and yellow and red tulips to provide the central interest.

Such comments are really missing the point of show work, which was never meant to be used at home, although, of course, exhibits may contain many ideas that can be adapted for home use. What is seen at flower shows is often exaggerated just for the show – if it were not and flower arrangements were always the same, no one would want to attend the shows. Structures are made especially for shows to hold flowers in odd positions, and clashing colours – which you would probably not want to use at home – are included in the schedule to test the exhibitors' appreciation of colour and its interpretation. The show schedule will make all kinds of demands to assess the competitors' knowledge of the principles of design and of suitability (to the title of the class) and will cover all aspects of the art of flower arranging. All kinds of conditions may be set out, most of which the casual observer will be unaware of, and the exhibitor must, of course, follow the precise wording of the schedule because all the conditions will be well known to the trained judges, who will base their decision on the following criteria:

- the *interpretation* of the title of the class
- the *design, scale* and *proportion*, which must conform to the space given
- the way in which *colour* is used to interpret the title of the class using plant material
- the *suitability* of the arrangement – that is, are the plant materials, accessories, bases and so forth suitable to the title?
- the *condition* of the plant material; this criterion should always be predominant
- whether there is some note of *distinction*

So, when a visitor at a show remarks that he or she hates a certain exhibit or would never have it at home, it must be remembered that the exhibitors are working to a difficult schedule and would probably not create such an arrangement for their own homes. Rather, the exhibitors are submitting their knowledge of the art of flower arranging to the testing eyes of the judges, just as ice skaters will slavishly follow the principles of correctly making the twists and turns during the figure sessions. Ice skaters are free to do as they please in the free creative sessions, and flower arrangers may do as they please when they pick and cut flowers for use in their own homes.

When you are at home, there is no show schedule to dictate how you use flowers. You might choose to arrange some sprays casually, as you have picked them in the garden. You might use a favourite vase or container time after time because you like it. You might create a colour scheme to suit your personality or to complement or contrast with the furnishings of the room in which the arrangement is to be placed. You might not follow any of the principles of design, placing the flowers in a wide-mouthed container filled only with water, certainly not using a little piece of floral foam that will have dried out by the following day.

In other words, what you do at home, whether you are using fresh or dried flowers, is to create an arrangement that pleases you. Just as when you look at the fashions in a magazine you are not expected to wear at home all the creations you see, although they may spark off ideas, so flower arranging competitions are not only meant to make the exhibitors try harder but they are also intended to inspire visitors into an awareness of the potential uses of plant materials that can be adapted for the home.

The national flower arranging societies or associations of most countries have very informative booklets for judges and competitors. Readers from countries without such national bodies can obtain information from: NAFAS, 21 Denbigh Street, London SW1V 2HF, UK.

Here I arranged mixed late summer flowers in a circular bowl on this beautiful antique table at Penshurst Place, Kent.

CHAPTER EIGHT

❀

Everlasting and Dried Flowers

$\mathcal{M}$ost of us love to have flowers in the home, but 'if only they would last' is the cry of so many. Well, of course, they will last if you grow and use many of the so-called everlasting flowers. In fact, there are several other flowers that can be dried and preserved successfully, and although I do not think that dried flower arrangements will ever take the place of a bowl of flowers freshly picked from the garden, they do have a decorative and useful role to play in parts of the home.

Some everlasting flowers can be easily grown from seed. One of my own favourites is the dainty *Acroclinium roseum*, which bears rose pink daisy-like flowers. It is a hardy annual and is quite easy to grow. Pick the flowers before they are fully mature, tie them up in small bunches and hang them upside down in a dry, airy place to dry out. The crisp, straw-like petals look really lovely in arrangements with blue *Statice sinuata*, which can be grown as an annual. Xeranthemums, which are sometimes also called immortelles, can be grown as annuals, and they have stronger stems than acrocliniums when they are dried.

Among the true everlasting flowers are helichrysums (straw flowers), which are invaluable for winter decorations. Try making a cushion of them by inserting short-stemmed flower heads into a pad of floral foam. This will look attractive on a dressing-table or a desk. You can hold the flowers firmly in place by inserting a pin down through the centre of the flower into the foam. If you want to use flowers with longer stems for an upright arrangement, you will find it easier if you give each flower head a false stem. Bend over one end of a length of wire to form a little crook (or you could use a thin hairpin), and insert the wire through the head so that the hook is caught in the centre of the flower and prevents the wire falling through. Cover the length of wire that is left with crêpe paper or with florist's tape to simulate a stem.

Always pick everlasting flowers before they are fully open. If you do not, they will continue to open when they are hung upside down to dry and might go to seed. I tried the new variety *Helichrysum bracteatum* 'Hot Bikini' last year, and its red flowers looked really striking arranged with the silvery seed capsules of honesty (*Lunaria*).

When they are dried, ornamental grasses give a delicate touch to many winter arrangements, whether of dried or fresh flowers. The seeds for these grasses, which are grown as hardy annuals, come in mixed packets, but it is possible to obtain separately the seeds of grasses such as squirrel-tail, greater quaking grass (*Briza*

Fill the top of the pot with floral foam to reach an inch (2.5cm) above the rim, then insert the tall grasses and glycerined beech leaves for height, making a downward swerve with Lonas *(everlasting yellow buttons) to form an irregular outline. Fill in with teazles, yellow achillea and helichrysum, each stem gradually shorter than the last. Add preserved leaves at the back.*

❀

maxima), golden foxtail (*Alopecurus pratensis* 'Aureo-marginata'), the browny-purple *Panicum virgatum* 'Rubrum' or even gardener's garters (*Phalaris arundinacea*). I love the nodding heads of *Briza maxima*, which look so effective when they are sprinkled with glitter for Christmas decorations.

The dried seedheads of love-in-a-mist (*Nigella*) can look extremely attractive when they are sprayed with gold paint. You can also paint them with clear varnish and shake the heads in a bag of glitter before the paint or varnish dries. Poppy seedheads can be decorated in the same way. In fact, all of the plants that can so easily be grown from seed can be treated like this – you can save money by shaking out the seeds to be sown the next year and making the seedheads into attractive winter decorations.

Several of the taller growing annual flowers can be dried well. Larkspur, love-lies-bleeding (*Amaranthus*), bells of Ireland (*Moluccella*), globe thistle (*Echinops*) and red orach (*Atriplex*) all dry well, but do not leave them in the garden until they are nearly over. Pick them before they are fully mature. Many of these, especially larkspur, I dry after picking by standing the stems in a jar of warm water mixed with glycerine (use one part glycerine to *five* parts water) for approximately 24 hours before hanging them upside down to dry. This treatment seems to keep the petals more firmly on the stems. If you want to keep the colours vivid, try adding a few spots of appropriately coloured ink or even a tiny amount of cold-water dye to the solution. I colour hydrangeas, bells of Ireland and love-lies-bleeding in this way, but I do not dry love-lies-bleeding by hanging it upside down as the tassels will dry like stiff pokers; instead I stand the cut stalks in a jar to dry so that the tassels hang downwards.

Globe thistles (*Echinops*) and other thistle-like flowers should be picked when they are young and either buried in silica gel (a powdered desiccant that is available from chemists) or sprayed with a clear lacquer. Hair lacquer will do, although craft and art shops stock a fine clear lacquer.

If you are new to drying flowers, begin with helichrysums, statice, acrocliniums and xeranthemums, together with some grasses. Then look around your garden for other flowers that might dry, for half the fun lies in experimenting. Look out for seedheads, too – you can have no idea how attractive the pale green seedheads of candytuft (*Iberis sempervirens*) can look in an arrangement.

This short chapter is not meant to go fully into the subject of dried flower decorations; I have written on this subject in other books. However, it is important to be able to preserve some sprays of leaves, which are needed in the background of some autumn and winter church decorations. Pick suitable branches of beech or other woody stemmed leaves. Wash the leaves to remove any dust, re-cut the stem ends and leave them standing in water overnight so that the channels are fully charged with water. Then mix a solution of one part glycerine to *two* parts hot water and stand the stems in the solution, leaving them until the leaves turn brown, which may take two or three weeks. The leaves are then preserved for all time.

Fill the dish with floral foam, insert tied bunches of wheat and add the cut stems (different lengths). Cover the foam with moss or short-stemmed flowers such as helichrysums and achillea. Tie the wheat round a short stick to give easier insertion into the foam.

HERE·LYETH·Yᴱ·RIGHT·NOBLE·AND·EX
LADY·IANE·GVYLDEFORD·LATE·DV
BERLAND·DAVGHTER·AND·SOLE·HEY
HONORABLE·Sᴿ·EDWARD·GVYLDEF⸱
WARDEYN·OF·Yᴱ·FYVE·PORTES·Yᵉ·W
WAS·SONNE·TO·Yᴱ·RIGHT·HONOR⸱
GVYLDEFORD·SOMETYMES·KNIGH
NION·OF·Yᴱ·MOST·NOBLE·ORDRE·O
THE·SAID·DVCHES·WAS·WYFE·TO·T
AND·MIGHTY·PRINCE·IOHN·DVDL⸱
OF·NORTHVBERLAND·BY·WHOM⸱
XIII·CHILDREN·THAT·IS·TO·WETE·V
V·DAWGHTERS·AND·AFTER·SHE·HA
XLVI·SHE·DEPARTED·THIS·TRANSIT⸱
HER·MANER·OF·CHELSEᵉY·XXII·DAYE⸱
Yᵉ·SECOND·YERE·OF·Yᵉ·REIGNE
VEREYNE·LADY·QVENE·MA
FIRST·AND·IN·A·ᵒMDLV
WHOSE·SOVLE·IESV·HAVE

Index